Political Parties

LIBRARY OF POLITICAL STUDIES

GENERAL EDITOR:
H. VICTOR WISEMAN

Professor of Government
University of Exeter

General editor's introduction

This series of monographs is designed primarily to meet the needs of students of government, politics or political science in Universities and other institutions providing courses leading to degrees. Each volume aims to provide a brief general introduction indicating the significance of its topic, e.g. executives, parties, pressure groups, etc., and then a longer 'case study' relevant to the general topic. First-year students will thus be introduced to the kind of detailed work on which all generalisations must be based, while more mature students will have an opportunity to become acquainted with recent original research in a variety of fields. The series will eventually provide a comprehensive coverage of most aspects of political science in a more interesting and fundamental manner than in the large volume which often fails to compensate by breadth what it inevitably lacks in depth.

James Jupp, who has already written on Australian parties, attempts in this volume to apply the general classification worked out for Western parties to those of developing countries. Party systems, internal party organisation, the influence of political, economic and social systems on parties are examined, with special reference to mass radical movements. He argues that programmes, ideologies and supporting interests must be taken into account in describing party systems. On the basis of his knowledge of Britain and Australia he has now paid particular attention to the 'third world', especially in Asia, and to totalitarian systems. This is a lively addition to the literature in this field and, together with the companion volume on *Pressure Groups* by Frank Castles, should be widely welcomed.

H.V.W.

Contents

CONTENTS

Preface

This book is an attempt to make some generalisations about political parties in a short enough form to be useful to the student. It is not intended as a substitute for detailed studies of particular parties nor for the classics in the comparative study of parties. Indeed its main aim is to draw attention to and comment upon, the work of others. My own contribution is largely that of extending the discussion of parties beyond the European and American systems and up to the present day. My basic proposition is that parties are indispensable to modern politics and that the absence of parties suggests that a system is governed by a traditional élite which has yet to come to terms with the modern world. From this point of view parties are neither good nor bad but simply necessary. Without them it would be impossible to legitimise modern systems, to engage the loyalty and support of the citizens. The alternative to party rule is either aristocracy or violent repression. Even under totalitarianism the party is able to mobilise mass support for the system while also using the weapons of terror. In all systems the party widens the area from which political leaders are recruited and is thus a 'democratising', if not necessarily a 'liberalising', force.

My own experience of and preference for party systems is confined to what I have called the 'Anglo-Scandinavian, distinct bi-partisan or social-democratic mode'. Part of my aim has been to assert the claims of this type of system to serious consideration, as against the more resolutely advanced claims of American sociology on the one hand and Soviet ideology on the other. However, as I argue throughout, party systems tend to be appropriate to certain social conditions and historical circumstances and cannot be artificially created simply because one likes them. Indeed, I believe that both American and Soviet advocates have often overlooked this fact when urging systems upon other nations. This personal position of mine needs stating to avoid any pretence of complete 'neutrality', something rather unattainable if not worthless, when writing about party politics.

My academic interest in parties was first aroused at the London School of Economics by Professors Mackenzie and Macrae while my experience of parties has been gained through the British and Australian labour movements. My colleagues at the Universities of Melbourne and York, and in the Political Studies Associations of Britain and Australia, have been valuable critics. My wife Helen has helped me to eradicate some of the literary effects of reading too much political jargon. Finally, I must thank Mrs. Ray Nixon for typing my manuscript so quickly and efficiently.

JAMES JUPP

1

Party systems

The notion of party has been with us since collective deliberation became institutionalised. There were parties in the Roman Senate, in medieval Italy and in the Tudor and Stuart parliaments. They may have been bound by family or clan loyalties, by social origin or by common attitudes. Whatever the basis, party rests on the acceptance of uniformity and co-operation by those engaged in collective deliberation. Thus it is possible to have parties within Churches or trade unions which are not identical with or even related to the institutions normally referred to as political parties. The distinguishing characteristic of the political party is that it has been brought together to influence or to control the political institutions of a society. A political party may have no chance of controlling the government of a country but if it has such control as a specific aspiration then it is entitled to be classed with parties which do exercise control. The party which merely influences must have the aim of some eventual control if it is not to be classed simply as a pressure group or sect.

Difficulties of definition

There are difficulties in the definition of party, not least in the distinction between party and pressure group. Many political movements, of which the most recent in Britain

I

has been the Campaign for Nuclear Disarmament, are something more than pressure groups but have deliberately eschewed eventual control of political institutions. These movements have a programme, a leadership and, frequently, a disciplined loyalty. They are content to leave the choice of representatives and of rulers to the established political parties. Once they abandon this self-abnegation they must become parties themselves. Similarly, interest groups like trade unions become or form political parties once they can no longer trust the established parties. A party based directly on an interest group is no less a party than one based on an ideology or a social élite.

Some of the confusion in defining party stems from the incomplete and socially or temporally determined definitions that have been used since parties became a normal feature of politics at the beginning of the nineteenth century. To Disraeli a party was a group of men banded together to pursue certain principles. This widely accepted definition only causes puzzlement when applied to loosely defined party systems in which no common fund of principles seems to distinguish one party from another. It does not help to explain why two parties may continue a separate existence when they have no major disagreements on issues. It leads to disillusionment or cries of 'the end of ideology' when previously distinct parties seem to be agreeing on more and more issues.

More recent definitions are often as much astray. To Marxists, political struggles are determined by the underlying class struggles. To Lenin and Stalin a party was a part of a class. The revolutionary proletarian party was to be the leadership of, and would be based upon, the industrial proletariat. Lenin modified this view by arguing that the working class, by its own efforts, was only capable of trade union consciousness. It could not spontaneously produce a correct leadership and this had to be brought to it from outside, by those who had mastered Marxism. Quite

2

apart from Lenin's modification, it is apparent that many parties are not based on classes, except in the rather tenuous sense that a majority of a social class may vote for one party in preference to another. Leninists have tried to solve this dilemma by arguing that non-Marxist 'working class parties' are objectively serving the interests of the bourgeoisie. This definitional juggling is hardly tenable. It is particularly difficult to sustain for the very large number of parties in the underdeveloped world which are clearly based on religions, tribes or language groups. All that it leads to is a scientifically spurious application of labels like 'national bourgeois' which are changed to 'progressive forces' when Soviet foreign policy demands it.

Nor can it be said that Western definitions are much less determined by the social environment from which they arise. American political sociology often seems blinkered by the peculiar and atypical American party system. There has been a tendency to deny the term 'party' to the totalitarian communist organisations which now govern one-third of the world's population. As Lasswell writes, in *The World Revolution of our Time*, 'For many purposes it is enough to define a political party as an organisation specialised with regard to presenting candidates and issues under its own name in elections. So conceived, the term "party" does not apply to the so-called "single" parties of the totalitarian régimes, since no true elections occur.' To some extent this limited view of party has been sustained by the structural-functionalist school of political scientists associated with Princeton University. Although dealing with the underdeveloped world more centrally than Lasswell, they still see parties as responsible for 'interest aggregation', as specialised bodies which should, in a modernised society, abstain from interference in administrative, judicial, or educational activities. Their function, ideally, is that of the American parties, to give coherence and direction to the pressures within society, to

3

provide a channel to power, but not to exercise true power themselves other than in controlling the legislature.

The notion of parties as channels to legislative authority for pressures does fit the American system extremely well. It becomes less satisfactory the further one moves from Washington. The word 'party' has passed almost unchanged into languages like Russian and Indonesian, and means something quite different from what it means in the United States. Competitive elections are engaged in by only one-third of the world's population, but parties exist in all but a handful of countries. One-third of the world's population is under direct party rule, with the legislature of little importance, with administrative, judicial, economic and educational functions directed by the ruling Communist Party, and with all institutions, from the unions and the Church to the army, subject to Party penetration and control. Clearly the party in the communist world is more powerful than in the competitive democracies. But is it any less of a party? The Soviet Communist Party started as one of many political parties in Tsarist Russia and as part of European social-democracy. The Chinese Communists began with only fifty members represented at their first Shanghai conference in 1921. Yet they are no less a party than the Kuomintang. They have hierarchy, an ideology and the aim of retaining the power which took forty years to win. It seems at least dubious to argue that a party which has always aimed at total power changes into some other species of organisation when it is victorious.

A useful definition of party is that of J. S. Coleman in *Political Parties and National Integration in Tropical Africa*, 'Political parties are associations formally organised with the explicit and declared purpose of acquiring and/or maintaining legal control, either singly or in coalition or electoral competition with other similar associations, over the personnel and the policy of the government of an actual or prospective sovereign state' (see p. 2). At

4

the simplest level then, any group of men, however organised, which calls itself a party, and which aims, however optimistically, at some degree of control over the
political institutions of its society, must be regarded as a
party. The institutions which it will seek to control will
vary with the system. In competitive democracies it may
well be satisfied with a majority, directly or in combination, in the legislature. In less stable or modernised
societies, the boundaries of party concern will be much
more blurred. Whatever the form of society, the ideological party, which wants an ideal system will not be
satisfied with a limited role, however much it may be
forced into such a role by the traditions of the society
in which it operates. The only compelling proof that a
'party' can be excluded from the category in which it
places itself, is that it consistently refuses to take the steps,
whether constitutional or revolutionary, which could
give it control over any of the recognised political institutions of its society. Thus the 'parties' in Church or unions
are excluded to the extent that they are only concerned
with controlling an interest group and have no further
aspirations. Size, structure and ideology are relatively unimportant in defining a party. Even the most obscure back-
street faction may console itself with the thought that
Hitler was member number seven in the Nazi Party. The
very small and powerless party may be termed a sect, if
its situation prevents it from carrying out the characteristic functions of parties.

Party systems

Because parties have become almost universal in this
century there are a wide variety of party systems or
arrangements of parties. Prior to 1917, the notion of a one-
party system was virtually unknown except very briefly
during the Jacobin phase of the French revolution. Today,
in contrast, a majority of countries of the world and nearly

5

two-thirds of its population are governed by single parties. Unless one denies the word party to these systems, as Professor Crick denies them the term politics in his *In Defence of Politics*, then there is obviously a growing need to inspect the broad category of one-party systems to see if there are any sub-categories, any differences of function or of structure amongst them. Quite apart from this new and expanding group of party systems, there is need for futher sophistication of the categories used since the beginning of the century. The distinction between two-party and multi-party systems is one which needs to be closely inspected. It gives rise to a number of false assumptions and futile enquiries, and must thus be suspect as a tool for political scientists. Is there anything in common between the American and British party systems, except that there are two major parties in each of them? This sort of dilemma gives rise to the kind of futile academic exercise found, for example, in Australia, where the system has been typified as two party, two-and-a-half party, three party, two-and-two-half party, and four party, without adding much to the literature of the subject.

To categorise party systems it is no longer enough simply to look at the number of parties involved, particularly as their emergence or decline may be caused by something as simple as changing the electoral laws. Political scientists have now got away from the simple numerical approach. Professor Almond, in *The Politics of the Developing Areas*, distinguishes four major categories with some subdivisions. These are 'authoritarian' (with a separate sub-category of totalitarian); 'dominant non-authoritarian'; 'competitive two party'; and 'competitive multi-party'; (working and *immobiliste*). While this is a great improvement on early schema, it still brackets together the British and American systems, gives too much credence to the notion that one party systems are of the same order as totalitarian systems, and ignores the differences in style, in party aspirations and in the effec-

6

tiveness with which parties carry out their functions.

Almond's broad typology is useful for his general purposes of discussing the modernisation process, the ways in which traditional societies are likely to develop their institutions, to specialise them and to separate out their functions. For a close study of parties as such, a few modifications seem called for. It seems quite impermissible, though almost universal among American political scientists, to place the North American and North European systems together as though they were almost indistinguishable. The structure of parties in the two systems is quite different. Their commitment to a programme varies in kind rather than in degree. The relationship of interest groups, particularly of business and labour, to the parties is quite different. Despite some appearance of convergence in the past twenty years, it must be strongly maintained that the whole style of American politics differs from that of politics in Britain, Scandinavia and Australasia. Not to recognise this is to succumb to the endless arguments as to whether a socialist movement is likely to emerge in America or to disappear in the Anglo-Scandinavian countries. This is primarily an ideological discussion, motivated by desire rather than by observation.

Categories of party systems must include not only numerical criteria but stylistic ones as well. When separating a totalitarian from an authoritarian system, for example, it is not enough to argue that the presence of minor parties is the deciding factor. Were that so, then East Germany would be less totalitarian than Yugoslavia which, at least by common Western acceptance, is not the case. The important factors include the degree of control over all aspects of life and the ideological approach to such control. In their desire to get away from the largely meaningless Left-Right scale of parties, political scientists have often got away from programmes and ideologies altogether; they have tended to overlook the style and content of party systems. Difficult though it may be to gauge adherence to programmes among politicians, some attempt to do so must be made. To class Britain together with the United States overlooks the institutionalisation of a radical collectivist philosophy in Britain and the organisational basis of one of the two parties in the trade unions.

A classification by party style

Party systems may be scaled from those in which discipline is loose, authority rests with the socially prominent and programmes are less important than immediate issues, to those in which discipline is rigid, authority rests with those recruited by the party, and ideology is central to the party's influence in all fields of human activity. This is simply a scale, and not a sequence. There is little reason to suppose that one system will change into any other, or even, over a century or more in a few cases, that it will basically change at all. A traditional society will not always create loose, non-programmatic parties, simply because this was the form of party which arose in the eighteenth century with the modernisation of Britain and the United States. Totalitarian parties will not necessarily become less disciplined and thus more likely to create competitive party systems, just because the trend to competition can be seen in Mexico or Turkey. All that is being said here is that, at present, those systems not in a state of complete chaos or dissolution at the time of writing, can be categorised usefully as a guide to the further discussion of parties.

Indistinct bi-partisan system

A first broad category is the *indistinct bi-partisan system* of which by far the most important example is in the United States. The American party system still reflects its origins at the end of the eighteenth century. There are no major programmatic differences between Democrats and
8

Republicans, though certain attitudes are more likely to be found among the adherents of one party than the other. Party discipline is loose in the legislature and virtually non-existent in the localities, though party loyalty is well regarded. The parties lack the formal hierarchical structure common to parties in most continents other than the American. Essentially the parties are alliances of local electoral committees, as they were both in Britain and the United States over a century ago. Central organs do exist, but their main concern is with propaganda rather than with the control of the party machine as a whole. The party has a leader, but it also has a number of strongly placed aspirants, who are quite free to campaign against him within the party confines and in full public view. None of this is to say that there are not life-long party loyalists, but rather that their efforts are not structured into a pyramid of power, nor their loyalties tied to a programme, as is the European tradition.

This type of party system tends to be dominated by the socially prominent, although it may create party leaders from the relatively obscure. American politics, especially the system of primary ballotting, encourages the wealthy. 'From log cabin to White House' is now less typical than 'from millionaire to White House'. In Congress, in Presidential conventions and in State capitals, the businessman, the corporation lawyer, the White, Anglo-Saxon Protestant, is favoured by both parties although more so by the Republicans. While the Democrats rely for much of their vote on labour and ethnic minorities, these have found it hard to rise to the top except in some big city machines where municipal rather than national office is held out. In all of this, as in some other respects, the American system is close to the Liberal-Conservative division of nineteenth-century Britain, also an *indistinct bi-partisan system*. Its influence as an example has been fairly limited.

Despite the existence of minor parties based on labour, farmers and French-Canadians, the party system of

Canada is basically indistinct, with the nineteenth century divisions between Liberals and Conservatives retained. Other American countries, most notably Uruguay, Colombia and Brazil, and, by colonial imitation, the Philippines, also have an indistinct two party system. While there are very important stylistic differences from the U.S. pattern, not least in the relative instability of democracy in Latin America, these all possess the characteristics of loosely disciplined, non-programmatic parties, based on the socially prominent. Similar systems may be emerging in Greece and Turkey, in the first case from the multi-party system, in the second from a one party system. However, the Greek party system was suspended by military coup in mid-1967 and will, presumably, not be restored in its previous form.

Distinct bi-partisan system

The second type of bi-partisan system is *distinct*. The parties have a clear, pyramidal structure and discipline, have continuing programmatic differences in the eyes of their members if not of the more jaundiced voters, and typically have substantial differences between the social composition of their élites. The major form of the *distinct bi-partisan system* is found in North-western Europe and its Australasian outpost. It seems reasonable to categorise Norway as a *bi-partisan distinctive system*, even though six parties are elected to its parliament. The crucial point is that only a combination between the still formally independent non-socialist parties can defeat the Labour Party. The same is true of Denmark, Sweden and Australia which have all been classed as distinctive bi-partisan systems although more than two parties are elected to the legislature. In this form, one of the major components is based on the trade unions and has a collectivist philosophy, while the other receives support from business, the professions and farming and has patriotic and individualist traditions, though increasingly modified by the influence of the social-democratic competitor. The parties are based on individual members who are expected to be disciplined in such matters as nomination for public office, public support for the party programme and leaders, non-co-operation with the rival party or its nominees, and payment of regular subscriptions or levies. While the conservative party is dependent on the socially prominent and the well-off for support and leadership, the labour party has been quite successful in elevating manual workers, in fact rather more successful than most other kinds of party. However, there is a tendency for these manual workers to have passed through the official positions of the union movement, or to have been educated out of their class.

Parties which are specifically based on interests in this way retain their distinctiveness even if their programmatic differences become less marked. Class loyalty in voting is more apparent than in the *indistinct systems* of North America, as R. R. Alford shows in his *Party and Society*. In those labour parties based on direct union affiliation, as in Britain, Sweden, Norway, Australia and New Zealand, an avenue to power for the organised working class is kept open as it is not by the simple application of pressure upon an *indistinct* party. Even in the independent social-democratic parties of West Germany, Japan, Austria or Denmark, the need to rely on union funds and loyalty keeps the door open. It is typical of this social-democratic variant of the *distinct bi-partisan system*, that the union movement is highly organised. Its membership coverage ranges from 90% in Sweden to 40% in Britain, as compared with 25% of the American labour force and rather less of the Canadian.

A minor variant of the *distinct bi-partisan system*, confined perhaps by imitation to the British Commonwealth, is that where the basis is not economic but social. Religion divides the two parties of Ulster, while race divides those of Guyana, Mauritius and Fiji. It could be argued that language divides the two parties of white South Africa, were it not that the distinctive differences between the Nationalists and the United Party have declined and an *indistinct party system*, which some see as merging into a one-party system, seems to characterise white South African politics. The distinctiveness of the parties here described does not necessarily derive from programmatic differences. The economic, religious or racial divisions presuppose a permanent clash of interests and it is not surprising that programmatic differences arise. That these are programmatic, concerned with immediate reforms, rather than ideological, concerned with an ideal society, should not blind us to the fact that they have a force in themselves, over and above party or group loyalty. It is easier to rationalise the clashes on which the *distinct party system* is based than to find reasons for disagreement within an *indistinct system*.

The remaining competitive systems may be described as the *multi-party* and the *dominant party* systems. These categories correspond to those used by Almond. In the *multi-party system* coalition politics are normal, often, but not always, based on parliaments elected by proportional representation. The structural-functional school tends to argue that the failure to resolve conflicts into a basic two-party division reflects on the uneven development of the society in its process of modernisation. This does not do credit to the internal strengths of party systems. While fluid, parties nevertheless attach loyalties to themselves which preserve their integrity against social changes, especially if the electoral system favours multiplicity. There is no clear sociological reason why Finland and Iceland should have multi-party systems while Sweden and Norway have essentially two-party confrontations if in a multi-party form. There seems no reason why the religious tensions of Holland, or the linguistic tensions of Belgium should not resolve themselves on the basis of a distinctive

12

two-party system. Nor is there any immediately apparent reason for Ceylon having a multi-party system while much of India has a dominant party system.

Multi-party system

Essentially, a *multi-party system* should have no permanent alliances, forcing a two-party confrontation. In the ideal situation, every partner should be capable of alliance with every other one. In Ceylon, for example, where there are normally about ten parties in the House of Representatives, every one of them has been involved in a coalition during the past five years. There are, of course, some alliances which are more likely than others. Some parties, usually communists or fascists, are normally left out, and coalitions, for example in Italy, tend towards the centre. Despite the compromises of coalition, the parties manage to retain their distinctiveness. They are normally based on mass membership, with hierarchies of command and discipline, but there will also be other variants. Whereas in the two-party systems the major parties tend to resemble each other in important organisational aspects, in the *multiparty system* the entire range of organisational types may be found.

Of all the competitive party systems the multi-party tends to be the most unstable and the one most likely to be overthrown. The Weimar Republic, the French Fourth Republic, Indonesia, pre-Fascist Italy, Congo, are often quoted examples of the weakness of multi-partyism. Perhaps the only really convincing proof of the durability of this type is in Israel, which, despite an almost unprecedented hostile encirclement, still supports the luxuries of proportional representation, many parties, and frequent coalitions and cabinet crises. Israeli unity is preserved by something other than the party system, which was not true of the larger polities mentioned above. Certainly no one would recommend a multi-party system for a newly-established country. The failure to build up permanent leaders of the nation, the constant compromise and frequent public defeats of the government are very bewildering for those with any sense of insecurity or even the mildest of authoritarian personalities. Essentially the *multi-party system* is attempting like all competitive systems to resolve conflict and demands. The difference is that it achieves this in public, while two-party systems are more likely to reach their compromises behind the closed doors of party meeting rooms.

Dominant party system

The *dominant party system* has developed in a limited number of countries, but it includes in India by far the largest of the systems in which competitive elections shape the composition of the legislature. Had India not been partitioned then it might have built up a two-party system based on Congress and the Muslim League. However, with the removal of this basis the only rivals to Congress have been parties which grew out of it and remain under its shadow. Even the Indian Communists were forced into Congress while outlawed by the British. The Socialists, Swatantra, Jan Sangh and nearly all the host of minor parties were founded by former Congressmen. In late 1966, various State Congress dissidents got together to form a People's Congress Party, the latest example of constant splitting off from the main party. In Ceylon, Malaya and Burma the same process was clear, though with different results. The Malayan system remains *dominant party*, with the breakaway Pan-Malayan Islamic Party functioning strongly in one State. In Ceylon the Sri Lanka Freedom Party broke from the United National Party in 1951, and now forms the core of the Opposition. In Burma, too, the Anti-Fascist People's Freedom League split into 'clean' and 'stable' factions in 1958, laying the foundation of a two-party system which was, however, abolished by military

14

coup. There is thus no reason to regard *dominant party systems* as other than competitive. They tolerate minorities and even give rise to them by fission from the major party. Moreover in India, Malaysia and Mexico, the federal basis of political institutions allows power in the provinces to parties which are completely overshadowed at the centre. The Indian National Congress, while still dominant in New Delhi, had lost control of the majority of Indian states by the middle of 1967.

The *dominant party system* may grow out of, or into, a *broad one-party system*. The two variants are most commonly found in the underdeveloped world, and seem suited to the task of creating national unity out of diverse and hostile groups, while at the same time preserving some degree of freedom of expression and of political manoeuvre. It is hard to conceive of Indian democracy being sustained so successfully and for so long except on the basis of Congress domination. The alternative, which already exists in the Indian states of Kerala and West Bengal, is a particularly unstable form of multi-partyism. Similarly, in Malaysia, the Alliance of the United Malay National Organisation, of the Malayan Chinese Association and of the Malayan Indian Congress, has been able to establish a dominant central position, bridging both the constitutional fragmentation of the federated sultanates and the social fragmentation of the three major races.

Broad one-party system

The *broad one-party system* varies considerably. The very distinction between a 'broad', a 'narrow' and a 'totalitarian' one-party system is often maintained only with difficulty and must always involve a detailed inspection of the parties concerned. All are, by definition, governing parties, and are thus in a position to enforce their hegemony by the use of the police, the army, cen-

15

sorship and the prisons. Being free from constitutional challenge, the single party is always likely to succumb to dictatorial temptations. Yet it would be unreasonable to group all one-party systems together, however much they may seem to overlap. The process of 'liberalisation', both in the communist world and in the military dictatorships of Latin America and the Middle East, is most likely to take place on the basis of movement from a narrow to a broad one-party system. The self-denial of the leaders of the Mexican Partido Revolucionaria Institucional, or of the Turkish Republican People's Party, in deliberately allowing separate parties to grow up, came slowly and is unlikely to be typical. Professor W. A. Lewis, in *The Politics of West African States*, argues that the single party is very unlikely to democratise itself, has totalitarian ambitions of fascist or communist inspiration, and is not even a good focussing point for building national unity. It is certainly true that the best-known of all African single parties, the Convention Peoples Party of Ghana, did move steadily towards totalitarianism and was eventually overthrown by a military coup, suggesting that it had not brought the national unity and meaningful direction that was its aim. There have been other examples, of which the carefully thought out system of President Nyerere of Tanzania is the latest, which show that a single-party state may have both competitive elections and relatively free discussion within the bounds of one party.

Whether a one-party system is categorised as 'broad' or 'narrow' will depend on the degree to which the elections are contested, the freedom allowed to factions within the party, and to organised groups outside it, the degree of public criticism allowed and the extent to which the party is open to mass members, rather than being a closed élite. Naturally a system may oscillate between these two, depending on the intentions of the controllers of the ruling party. Thus in Paraguay, which

16

has been under the dictatorial control of the Colorado Party since 1928, there were free municipal elections for the first time in 1965, with opposition parties and newspapers allowed to function. It was the conscious desire of the communist leader Gomulka that Poland become a 'broad' one-party system. In its last two general elections contested seats have become normal, although all nominations must be made through the Communist-controlled National Unity Front. The Tanzanian system was consciously designed to prevent the abuses of the *narrow one-party system* and all but six seats were contested in the September 1965 elections even though all candidates were endorsed by the Tanzanian African National Union.

Narrow one-party system

The *'narrow' one-party system* also has vaguely defined boundaries. The single party may simply be a disguise for a military junta or a narrow traditional élite. It may have totalitarian aspirations which it is not efficient enough to carry through, but which obscure its true methods of operation. In small, underdeveloped states the narrow single party simply shades off into the personal clique of the dictator and is scarcely a 'party', in the sense of a collective group with a life and internal ethos of its own. On the other hand, in large states like Yugoslavia, the narrow single-party is in the process of broadening, has a vigorous internal life and is prepared to allow deviations from its directives. The militarily inspired parties of Egypt, Algeria or Burma may develop in a similar direction, particularly as all three countries have had some experience of conventional parties in the past. What really distinguishes the 'narrow' single-party from the 'broad' is that it does not allow contested elections nor encourage any form of opposition. Like the 'broad' party, its operation varies in accordance with the outlook of its leaders.

Totalitarian system

The final type of party system, the *totalitarian*, needs fuller description, and this is given in Chapter 6. There is general agreement among American political scientists about the broad features of totalitarianism, although there remain grounds for disagreement about the categorisation of any particular system. In particular there has been some disquiet, not least among Communists, about the classing together of Nazi Germany and the U.S.S.R. as the only 'ideal types' of totalitarianism. However, given the fact that the Nazi and Stalinist systems reached their height at the same time, and that German and Russian political ideas have fed off each other throughout this century, the common classification does not seem untenable. There is no reason why the ideologies of totalitarianism should be identical, any more than the ideologies of other types of party system. There is also no reason why parties ostensibly supporting the same ideology should be placed in the same bracket. Totalitarian parties may no more live up to their aspirations than do others. On the basis of contested elections, factional discussion, the existence of critical groups and journals and the continuation of private enterprise in agriculture, it seems unreasonable to group Poland and Yugoslavia together with the Soviet Union. It was not universal to regard Fascist Italy and Nazi Germany as identical systems. Today there is increasing variety in the Communist world.

Difficulties of categorisation

There are now over one hundred party systems functioning, and rather more if regional variations in federal systems are included. There remain some states where traditional élites still exercise power on an ascriptive basis, without the use of parties. Even in this declining group of un-Westernised, traditional societies, parties may exist

18

underground by foreign inspiration, or be formed in universities or schools by Western imitators. In some 'traditional' societies, Thailand for example, social arrangements are as complex and 'modern' as in many states which do have parties. Yet the Thai authorities have decided for the time being that they can do without this particular institution. Whether a country has no parties, one party or many parties is much more a matter of choice than determinists give credit for. While it is generally true that a modernised society, with a high living standard, high urbanisation and general literacy, is likely to sustain a competitive party system, there is nothing like the simple relationship which writers like Lerner or Coleman seem to assume. Whether a state has a two-party or a multi-party system bears little apparent relationship to its degree of modernisation or even of social cohesion. Duverger is closer to the truth when he relates the number of parties to the choice of electoral systems. Both France and West Germany have noted this relationship and now have election systems designed to reduce the number of effective contestants.

Over half the political systems operating today have been established in the past twenty years. Most of the others have been disrupted and reconstituted by war and revolution since 1914. European influences and example have shaped all the party systems now in existence. The *indistinct bi-partisan systems* of the American continent resemble in form the European party systems of the early nineteenth century. European colonialism has spread metropolitan example throughout the undeveloped world. The Soviet model has been consciously emulated and copied with modifications from Cuba to China. Cultural diffusion blurs the distinctions between party systems and makes categorisation perhaps more difficult than for other kinds of political institution. Much of contemporary political ideology is concerned with the functions, structure, composition and aims of the party. Thus parties tend to be more consciously shaped and directed by human desires than do bureaucracies or legal systems. This becomes less true as the party becomes an institution itself, with traditions and practices which are handed down within an established framework. All parties, however directive, are shaped by their societies. Societies may also be shaped by their parties.

Imitation, conscious direction and the gap between aspiration and achievement, all help to blur the distinctions between one party system and another. All the categories outlined above merely enclose a system at the time of writing. However, certain possibilities for future change may be assumed from the categorisation, though these are not probabilities. One would expect party systems to become less rigid the longer they are established, to move from the totalitarian towards the indistinct two-party end of the scale. This movement need not, however, be regular. It may be delayed or reversed. Permanent party systems have a habit of being shaped at certain crucial times in the history of the nation, and then of changing their nature very slowly. The United States party system is only just emerging from the lines drawn by the American Civil War, lines broad enough to accommodate industrialisation, massive immigration, and the rise to world power. The indistinct Irish system still has its lines drawn by the Treaty of 1921, as does its more distinctive Ulster counterpart. In Britain, the First World War and its accompanying effects of Liberal schism and massive trade union recruitment created the boundaries which still determine the struggle today. If the new and unstable systems of the underdeveloped world become established, they will probably reflect for many years the dominant position of the party under which freedom was gained, whether that dominance is expressed in competitive or one-party form.

When change does occur, other than by invasion or revolution, one would expect it to be between closely

20

related categories. If Communism becomes liberalised it will be by transition from the totalitarian to the narrow and then the broad one-party system. If competitiveness comes to the underdeveloped countries it will be by broadening the one-party system into a dominant party one, and then by schism into a two- or multi-party system, depending probably on the homogeneity of the society in other respects. A multi-party system, if it is not over-thrown or repressed for its divisiveness, may grow into a two-party system. The forces at work may include changes in the electoral system, the consolidation of coalitions along radical-conservative lines or the lessening of tensions be-tween different segments of the society. These gradual shifts in established, 'effective' party systems are less likely to occur in unstable, 'ineffective' systems where military or civil revolution is the normal agent of change. In an 'ineffective' system the parties do not exercise any real control over government although still permitted to exist. Such control is normally exercised by the armed forces.

2

Party functions

Party systems have been found necessary throughout most of the world and would arise in nearly all the remainder if they were not administratively discouraged. This suggests that parties have essential functions in all non-traditional political systems. These functions are generally discussed in three broad ways, the functionalist, the interest-serving and the enumerative. On the level of grand theory, structural-functionalist political scientists in the United States have seen parties as aggregating interests, setting goals and formalising conflict. Thus they are essential to the continued functioning of societies by resolving strains on social organisation and by legitimising governments. There is nothing unsound about this approach so long as it is freed from the crude determinism which argues that specific forms of party or party systems are necessarily appropriate to particular societies and must always arise in them. This does not take into account the vital role of cultural diffusion in the area of party politics. Most systems borrow and copy from each other and are not determined solely by their own society. Moreover, parties (unlike families or religion) have proved very vulnerable to repression. There is often no reason for the form a party system takes other than that the rulers of a state have consciously decided that such a form will be adopted. The social tensions resolved by one method may equally be resolved by another. The choice of method rests with the political leaders. Even in such a liberal environment as the United States itself, the form of party organisation has been preserved by laws about the conduct of primary elections, the registration of parties, access to the ballot paper, party finance and registration of voters which either do not exist in Europe or have long been abandoned. In Britain and France the restrictions imposed by government on the use of broadcasting time may be seen as encouraging some parties within the system, while in most states using proportional representation there are regulations which discourage minor parties. Thus a purely determinist approach can lead to misunderstanding of the varied possibilities within a party system. In particular, the tendency to argue that democratic forms cannot survive in underdeveloped societies crumbles against the fact that as many people live under competitive democracy in the 'third world' of Asia, Africa and Latin America as in the advanced countries, and that the most destructive form of totalitarianism ever to arise did so in one of the world's most industrialised nations. The great majority of non-competitive systems are in the underdeveloped world, but are also in small, almost non-viable polities which find difficulty in establishing any stable system.

Grand theory is useful in a general way for analysing societies but is dangerous when applied to particular historic situations. On the second level of abstraction it is possible to argue that certain types of party necessarily serve the interests of certain sections of society. This is the approach of most Marxists. Again, it leads to misleading determinism when applied to actual situations but can be fruitful in general. It is a particularly important contribution of this general approach that the élites or interests favoured by certain parties are studied, and the effects of interests on policy formation are taken into account. Thus a party which calls itself socialist but is

PP—C   23 totally dominated by the professional or business classes is likely to behave in a different way from one based on the trade union movement and drawing part of its leadership from the manual workers. A peasant party led by lawyers may have a different orientation from one led by farmers. The same truisms can be applied in studying the electoral bases of parties. Even if a party is led substantially by aristocratic and upper-middle classes, their interests must be compromised by those of the middle- or even working-class voters who return the party to office. The British Conservative Party is an obvious case in point. Thus a theory based on the serving of interests is more complicated than most Marxists suppose, but still fruitful. The basic assumption is that different social and occupational groups conceive of themselves as having conflicting interests and try to express these through the parties.

Parties may thus be seen as essential to the continued functioning of political society and also as expressing the demands of particular interests. The two broad approaches need not be contradictory if linked by a theory of the necessity of conflict for social cohesion. But in certain situations, especially those where revolutionary parties are involved, the expression of conflict may destroy the political institutions. It is at this stage that the arbitrary interference of government normally prevents the uncontrolled extension of disruptive political movements. It may do so at a very early stage, as most ruling communist parties have done, at a late stage, as General de Gaulle did in 1958, or after the battle has already been lost, as in Kuomintang China. The party becomes an agency for changing political institutions which no longer fulfil their function of social integration and the legitimisation and accomplishment of social goals. Society is remoulded by the newly victorious party which, in its turn, is influenced by the society which it has begun to command. Thus, in stable and fully legiti-

24

mised societies the parties essentially contribute to cohesion by channelling discontents and demands towards the agencies of government. In disintegrating, malfunctioning systems, however, a party can just as reasonably be seen as the instrument for changing the other political institutions. The extent to which it is able to do so will be determined by the ability of other alternative centres of authority, such as the army, to stop it from succeeding.

Below these levels of broad generalisation it is possible to enumerate a number of specific functions which parties may fulfil and to measure parties and party systems against these standards. Again, as at the level of broad generalisation, it is not tenable to argue that all parties must necessarily fulfil certain functions. By the definition adopted at the outset, parties must be avenues to power, however unlikely it is that they will be used. The extent to which a party is important for winning political office determines whether it is to be studied as a working part of the political institutions or simply as a sect, with appeals other than those of attaining power. The more stable and fully legitimised a political system, the easier it is to distinguish the sects from the parties. The essential difference is that the party has some access to office, however small, that it can place some of its adherents, however few, into positions of power within the recognised political institutions. Thus social-democracy is a sect in the United States, communism is a sect in Eire, liberal-democracy, if it exists, is a sect in the communist world, and anarchism must be a sect everywhere unless it modifies its principles as the Syndicalists did in Spain during the Civil War.

Patronage and control

As all parties are concerned with power they naturally operate by placing members and supporters into positions of power. Thus there is nothing derogatory in saying that a primary function of parties is patronage. In competitive democracies today, parliamentary positions are normally paid and normally dependent on party approval. The party leaders, however formally selected, are also the parliamentary leaders. Even in the British system, where patronage has always been a term of contempt, paid parliamentary posts are an example of the patronage role of parties. In the United States, where patronage has always been an essential feature of politics, far more posts are dependent on party approval than is the case in most other competitive systems. As the party system and the notions of discipline and membership are looser than elsewhere, this has not created the undemocratic machine-controlled situation which Ostrogorski foresaw at the beginning of the century. Nevertheless it is difficult to understand the American party system without placing patronage firmly at the centre of party functions. In other systems the patronage may be more noticeable in honorific positions such as local councillors, the peerage or appointments to ambassadorships. In the state controlled economies of most nations an element of party patronage in appointments to administrative and economic posts is extremely important. As previously in the United States, this may interfere with efficiency and with the professionalism of the bureaucracy. However, it is an essential element in maintaining party loyalty in poor countries where many livelihoods depend directly on government employment. Patronage may extend down from appointments to political or semi-political positions to the allocation of manual jobs, of state housing, of land and business permits.

The degree of party patronage varies to the extent that agencies other than government offer avenues for employment, or with the ethic of public life in the particular society. Where government employment is widespread and nepotism and patronage traditionally sanctioned, as in many underdeveloped countries, then parties naturally take over the role of patron from the aristocratic élites. This tendency was just as apparent in early nineteenth-century England as it is in Africa today, although the range of jobs open was smaller in a *laissez-faire* society. In the United States patronage had rather different origins. To some extent it merely continued earlier British practices. But it also reflected a democratic and populist tradition which held that the largest possible number of positions should be subject to election. Once parties came to dominate the electoral process, patronage naturally followed. During the mass immigration between 1860 and 1920, it came to be extended to manual jobs and poor relief, often on the basis of traditions from non-American social systems such as the Irish or the Italian. The big city machines relied on patronage in exchange for voting and other forms of support. Only with the spread of affluence and the professionalisation of bureaucracies did machines based on patronage start to lose their central role in the parties.

In the Soviet Union and other totalitarian countries, patronage is essential in maintaining control over society. The Soviet Communist Party today is an even more important patronage party than the Democratic Party of America ever was. However, the relationship with the beneficiaries is a different one. Their votes are not important and their loyalty is expected as part of the obligations of party membership. The Soviet *nomenklatura* system, supervised by the Central Committee, is part of the general system of control imposed by the official ideology. If the Communist Party is to lead society, then it can do so by appointing, controlling and disciplining the entire élite. The pragmatic and undisciplined American parties could never aspire to anything similar. The combination of patronage and control is essential to totalitarianism, though carried through less vigorously in Nazi Germany and Fascist Italy because of the support which existing

27

élites gave to the fascist movements. In most one-party systems there is a strong element of this combination. Employment depends on party loyalty. The opposite trend can be seen in Britain, where patronage is uncommon in paid positions. There a Labour government can appoint Conservatives to lead their Prices and Incomes Board and the Steel Board. In the British system nomination to official positions is often based on social or educational characteristics, rather than on party patronage. This makes it very difficult for a party to achieve its aims through the control of such appointees, even assuming the party to have closely defined goals. The party must try to rule through the conventions of ministerial control, with a party nominee as Minister at the head of each government department supervised through the parliamentary party and criticised by the party in the country.

Apart from patronage in government appointments, parties also employ their own staffs who, in Max Weber's term 'live off politics'. The Soviet Communist Party has the largest full-time staff in the world. With only eleven million members it employs directly some 200,000 officials. This compares with less than 2,000 agents and organisers co-ordinating the three million members of the major British parties. The difference reflects the limitation of competitive parties to electioneering, fund raising and propaganda. Even in the European parties, with their wider range of newspapers and greater control of trade union posts, the number of appointments directly dependent on the parties is fairly small. In the United States, where employment is usually by individual politicians and candidates, and where the amount of money available is far greater, the parties indirectly employ rather more people. However, these are not party officials in the European sense and have little direct policy-making role in the party, however important they may be for propaganda and public relations. In competitive party systems politics is still the province of amateurs. Michels

28

drew attention fifty years ago to the leading role of paid professionals in controlling the ostensibly democratic socialist parties of Europe. This is undoubtedly still the case, and must be while professionals have daily access to each other and to party records while the membership is scattered and meets spasmodically if at all. But at the electioneering and local levels competitive parties still depend on voluntary effort even in the age of mass communication and decision making by professional experts.

Setting and attaining goals

Most parties view their patronage function as in some way related to the attainment of political goals. All parties accept philosophical positions however vague and however unrelated to their actual functioning. The party philosophy provides an incentive to the amateurs who do not require or expect patronage. That parties are 'organised opinion' to some extent is undeniable. The force of this attribute is hard to measure. It is obvious in the American case, where cross-voting in the legislature is permitted, that members of the same party may not subscribe to the same specific programme or even the same values. This is obscured by more disciplined systems but can be ascertained by opinion polling. Most social-democratic parties contain the range from liberals to revolutionary socialists. Most conservative parties have extremists and moderates. The gap between the right-wing conservative Monday Club and the left-wing Labour *Tribune* in British politics is often as great as in West European politics but is contained within party structures dominated by more moderate parliamentary leaders. The commitment of party members cannot be effectively measured by a content analysis of official propaganda alone. Appeals are often tailored to the uncommitted rather than to the party. Even in totalitarian societies there is a great gap between what the party officially says and what many of its

29

members actually think, despite years of indoctrination. A second difficulty in judging the importance of ideals to a party is that what seems ideological and irrational to one person is commonsense and self-evident to another. European social-democrats regard the welfare state as pragmatic and uncontroversial while American conservatives regard it as communistic. The problem of value judgement is most acute when studying the importance and content of political ideology. It is true that parties need an ideology but equally true that they may be unaware of this need.

Terms like 'pragmatic' and 'dogmatic' must be treated carefully. There was little pragmatic about Senator Goldwater and little dogmatic about Professor Liberman, the Soviet economic reformer. Generally speaking, however, one can distinguish between ideological, programmatic and adjustive parties. This division corresponds with the party's generally accepted view of its relationship with society. Parties relate themselves positively or negatively to their societies. Positively related parties are primarily interested in patronage, in adjustment of interests, in preserving existing institutions, in creating social harmony. They are essentially conservative in the broad sense and dominated by satisfied social groups, at least among their leadership. The American parties correspond most closely to this model. They are adjustive, they do not require adhesion to the party programme nor discipline to achieve it. The programmatic party tends to be intermediate between a negative and a positive relationship to society. It wants to change basic institutions and social arrangements and caters for dissatisfied elements, labour, the poor and minorities. But it accepts the political framework in which it operates. Social-democracy is the archetype of the programmatic party, moving from a negative to a positive relationship with society. The negatively related party is naturally revolutionary, rejects existing arrangements and adopts a detailed and messianic philosophy to rationalise its discontents. It is what Smelser calls 'value-oriented' whereas the programmatic party is 'norm-oriented'. There is, then, a correspondence between the degree of ideological rigidity and comprehensiveness, and the extent to which a party is ready to work within existing institutions. This generalisation holds only for multi-party systems. In totalitarian societies the party turns its negativistic ideology into a philosophy of command. It becomes conservative in defence of existing arrangements while holding the monopoly on decisions to innovate.

Parties, whether adjustive, programmatic or ideological, all have the function of setting values for their societies and trying to attain them in concrete form. The adjustive party is essentially defending what already exists and what is usually fully legitimised and accepted by the great bulk of citizens as self-evidently sound. It can only be successfully challenged when a powerful enough segment of society rejects the established political values and feels alienated enough to launch a value-oriented movement. Almond and Verba's studies in the 'civic culture' suggest that this is unlikely in most advanced industrial nations which are heavily urbanised. However, sections like French-Canadians and Negroes may not be effectively integrated into the general civic culture and may be more available for challenging the adjustive philosophy. Programmatic parties rather more consciously attempt to change social values and goals. Over a generation or so a successful programmatic party may hope to shift the centre of political agreement in its direction, while remaining immune to rival creeds. People who do not consciously adhere to the party and even oppose it will come to accept its programme, will even press the other parties to accept the basic tenets. This has largely been the history of the social-democratic mode of politics in Britain, Scandinavia and Australasia in this century.

The ideological party is in the category of secular religion.

It attracts supporters for the same reasons as messianic creeds. It works for utopia both before and after attaining office whether with or against the wishes of those it is trying to save. There is much debate about the extent to which ideological parties will force events to fit their ideas, rather than being disguised pragmatists. To some extent, even ideologies are rational and will adjust to situations which are unavoidable. The ideology of governing parties is steadily emptied of content until it can cover all eventualities. The same is true, over longer periods, of religious denominations. However, the degree of coercion likely to be used for ideological and apparently impracticable ends can be substantial. While some glimmerings of rationality have been found for Stalin's disastrous programme of collectivisation, none have yet been adduced for Hitler's 'final solution'.

The effectiveness with which parties carry out their function as goal setters and attainers varies directly with their commitment to ideas. The adjustive party always shares this role with other institutions. Religious denominations, educational institutions, mass media and the bureaucracy will all be rivals for the role of goal-setters, attitude formers and political motivators. The adjustive party accepts the legitimacy of this rivalry and is unconcerned with it. The programmatic party may be more uneasy. It will set up rival mass media, build its own educational system, try to act as a secular religion, and insulate its members from the society as a whole. It can only achieve this to a limited extent compared with the ideological party. Its attitude towards society is increasingly positive as it is allowed to function freely and with some measure of success. The whole history of social-democracy is littered with 'socialist Sunday schools', newspapers, banners, rallies, cultural associations, propaganda campaigns. These attempt to set goals for society and may be fairly successful in shifting the centre of debate. However, no party which does not wish to restructure society,

32

by force if necessary, can ever replace its rival goal setters completely. Only the ideologically committed can do that.

Representation of interests

The claim that parties represent interests has been most fully elaborated by Marxists but was already evident to others before Marx died. An interest implies a claim on society made by a group of people however constituted. The claim may be simply to be left in peace, as with religious or ethnic groups. It may be for more money, as with economic interests. It may be for access to political power, as for the business community in England in 1832, or for nationals in colonial situations. In all cases the group concerned is seeking a political solution and will normally use parties for achieving its ends. Some interests are permanent, like labour and capital. Others are temporary, like residents in the path of a motorway or airlane. In the former case parties are likely to incorporate the interest while in the latter they are simply channels for the immediate protest. This 'aggregation of interests' is one of the most important functions of parties, because it reduces the strain on society by giving the aggrieved an outlet through which amelioration of the condition can be attained. This is certainly true for parties in competitive situations but in one-party states the party will distort the effects of pressures by choosing those which it wants to relieve and rejecting others.

Permanent interests become incorporated into the party system by electoral attraction, by elevation to party leadership, by organisational affiliation, by regular association, usually with a financial link, or by the actual creation of a party. Thus the Catholic Church, as an interest, created the 'confessional' Christian Democratic Parties of Europe, just as the unions created labour parties and as armies are now creating mass fronts. This is the most

33

obvious method for dealing with interest pressures. However, it does commit the interest to one party and limit its freedom to deal with others except through the chosen political instrument. The expectation is that voters enrolled in the interest will sustain the party. Clearly this does not apply mechanically. In Italy, which is over 95% Catholic, less than 50% support the Christian Democratic Party. In Sweden, with 90% of workers enrolled in unions, only 48% support the Social Democratic Party. The problem of unionists who vote conservative is faced by all labour parties. Only in conditions where a religious denomination is a large minority is it able to preserve solidarity. Thus the Catholic party in Holland gets a larger proportion of the co-religionist vote than Catholic parties in Belgium, Austria or Italy. This form of aggregating interests is most effective where the interest has a clear formal structure of its own, as unions and churches do. It is almost impossible to form a party based on consumers, unless they are enrolled in co-operatives, or on youth, or the poor, or the old. These categories may have interests but they have not organised them and are thus politically ineffective.

Apart from physically basing the party organisation on interests, the most common methods of incorporation are by the elevation of certain groups to power and by the attraction of votes from certain sections. In many underdeveloped countries the leaders choose themselves from existing élites or from the educated. The same is true to a large extent of advanced countries too. But some parties have been the chosen avenue to power for certain classes and sections. Manual workers have reached office in Britain almost exclusively through the Labour Party, Jews and Catholics in the United States largely through the Democrats, English-speakers in South Africa through the United Party. This tendency for parties to favour certain interests is even apparent in one-party situations. There was an excessive proportion of Georgians in the

34

Soviet Communist Party while Stalin and Beria were alive and it dropped quickly after 1953.

The capturing of an electoral base by a party makes it susceptible to claims by that section of society. However, a purely pressure-group theory of party policy making is untenable. Party leaders may not be drawn from the same classes as their supporters. Organised interests exert more pressure than the unorganised voter. Groups incorporated within the party structure have better access than those outside it. In bi-partisan systems the parties reach out to a broad range. They do not want to be known as tied to particular interests even though many of their voters support them for that reason. Social bases shift and the parties must follow them or be stranded. This is particularly true of parties with rural followings but it is also becoming true for parties based on manual occupations in advanced industrial nations. As the parties try to become 'national' rather than 'sectional' the influence of their loyal adherents may decline. Nevertheless parties will still represent interests to a major extent. Without the financial and electoral support of large social and economic groups the competitive party systems would become very confused and unstable.

3

Structure of parties

The structural form a party adopts is very closely related
to its functional and ideological emphasis. A revolutionary
party will adopt a structural form which would be irrele-
vant to the interests of a parliamentary party. A radical
party will give more emphasis to internal party democracy
than a conservative party based on the acceptance of
hierarchy. A party which depends on its supporters for
most of its funds will tend towards a more elaborate
structure and a larger enrolled membership than one
which gets donations from outside its ranks. Once a party
has become institutionalised it inherits the structure of its
pioneers to some extent. Some of the features of social-
democratic parties no longer serve a useful function for
electioneering because they were initially intended to
incorporate trade unions into the decision-making structure, in exchange for their political funds. Conservative
parties have everywhere found it difficult to broaden their
basis in order to attract voters no longer impressed by
aristocratic or élitist status alone. The more complicated
a party structure is, the more difficult a party finds it to
make changes in accordance with changing functions and
circumstances. The liberalisation of the communist movement has been delayed by adherence to 'democratic cen-
tralist' practices which seriously inhibit free debate within
the party. In less stable systems these problems of institu-

tional conservatism are not so acute. Whole parties may be abolished or reformed very quickly, especially where they have only been loosely connected committees dependent on socially prominent individuals. The African situation is the most fluid at present. In contrast, in Europe, North America and Australasia, party forms have continued essentially similar to those of fifty or even one hundred years ago. Within those forms practices may have changed. But the partisan has to operate within the machine and does not have the freedom to manoeuvre present in less entrenched systems.

The most detailed work on party structures is that of Duverger for Europe and of R. T. Mackenzie for Britain. Both reveal the complexity of organisation which modern mass parties have created. Duverger makes it clear that even within a single party system there is room for great variety of organisation. Mackenzie stresses for Britain what is also true of other two-party systems, that similar situations produce similar structural arrangements. In France there is a great range from the loose party of 'notables' to the highly-disciplined Communist Party. In Britain, in contrast, the arrangements of both parties are now basically similar, having developed from fundamentally different premises. Thus one has to take into account not only the objectives which the party sets itself, but also the needs dictated by the system within which it operates. A parliamentary party trying to operate in a revolutionary situation is futile, as the history of the Russian Social Revolutionaries and Mensheviks underlines. Equally a revolutionary party is liable to constant futility, as many West European communist parties show quite clearly. The attempt by the Communist International to impose a uniform technique on all member parties regardless of their situation, marks the most costly and frustrating failure to understand this point. One of the great difficulties which advisers from advanced countries face today is their attachment to their own styles of party.

37

Americans attempt to set up indistinct two-party systems, based on presidential rule, patronage and a depoliticised trade union movement. Sometimes, as in the Philippines, they are successful. British advisers often try to form labour parties based on unions and co-operatives. Sometimes, as in Singapore, their example may be copied with profit. The Russians foster monolithic single parties, the Chinese revolutionary guerilla parties, the Yugoslavs broad national fronts. Throughout the underdeveloped world one finds political movements which do not seem appropriate to their environment and which often wither away as a result. Usually they have been based on a model which was ideologically attractive but which was not organisationally appropriate.

The range of organisations

In some systems, then, parties may approximate to each other's structure, in others they may be derived from quite different models. Thus a scale of organisational types may apply within one nation or not. Such a scale corresponds to some extent to the party's ideology. The more messianic it is, the more it tends towards the rigidity and total mobilisation of totalitarianism. The more conservative the party, the more it relies on the established élites for leadership and funds, the less it adopts the features of a mass movement. In societies where political modernisation has not yet taken place, party labels may simply be attached to family groupings; this was true of the now defunct Nepal Congress.

The 'notable-led' party

The loosest form of organisation is that where the local élite simply functions as a party, attracting support to itself on the basis of traditional loyalty. This form of organisation was apparent in the shires and small boroughs

of England before the 1832 franchise reform and lingered
on in rural Conservative areas for one hundred years
longer. Rural areas are most likely to produce this type
of party, which Duverger has called the 'party of notables'. In rural France the parties still have this form,
even when ostensibly they have been amalgamated into
the Gaullist movement. In March 1965, M. Frey, French
Minister of the Interior, told the first national conference
of the Gaullist U.N.R. that it should aim at becoming 'an
organised party on the Anglo-Saxon model'. Thus even
in modernised industrial societies, a large rural basis
tends to perpetuate the party of notables. This has been
just as true for the United States, where an electoral bias
in favour of rural areas was one of many factors sustaining
loose party organisation. The integrated hierarchical mass
party is a product of urban politics.

The loose-associational party

Parties of notables deriving support from rural areas pre-
dominate in those underdeveloped countries with competitive systems. In India the strength of caste has meant that
the notion of family loyalty can be extended to a large
proportion of the people. Even anti-caste parties like the
Communists have been forced to depend on extended
families like the Reddis in Andhra or the Ezhavas in
Kerala. Within Congress itself the local and State digni-
taries have come to dominate the machine, replacing the
cosmopolitan and urban leaders of the independence
struggle. The characteristic feature of all such arrangements is that the party formalises traditional support but
does not effectively supplant this by loyalty to the party.
Party membership, where it exists at all on a formal dues-
paying basis, is needed for organising electoral campaigns
when opposition threatens. This is not as important as
the support which is already secured to candidates by
virtue of their family background or standing in the com-

PP—D   39

munity. The party may simply set up youth wings or some similar arrangement, to provide drivers or body-guards for the politicians. They will not give such broad organisations a true policy-making role. Policy will remain completely in the hands of the élite, who will be reluctant to submit completely to central direction. Thus parliamentary parties based on the 'notable' form of organisation tend to be indisciplined and factional. In the United States a loose associational characteristic has continued even into the present urbanised politics, though there are many other factors than localism which sustain it. In France, and to some extent Italy, industrialised countries have continued to support large 'notable' sectors based on rural politics. The factionalism which is an inherent feature of the Japanese Liberal Democratic Party is similarly based. However, in these increasingly urbanised countries it is more meaningful to describe parties as 'loose associational' rather than 'notable led'.

Parties based on rural support tend to be loosely integrated, indisciplined and élitist rather than hierarchical. The leaders chose themselves on an ascriptive basis and finance their own campaigns. They are thus free from obligations to the centre and are particularly likely to press for patronage on a local or family basis. However, as urban influences increase, or as ideologically based models are introduced from abroad, parties tend towards a more coherent and disciplined method of mass organisation. This is even true for the United States since the rise of the great city machines in the 1890's and the increasing importance of national politics since the 1930's. However, the development has been much slower in the Americas than in Europe. In both Britain and Germany, mass political machines had begun to grow by the 1880's and in virtually all industrialised countries outside the Americas, the hierarchically structured and integrated mass party is the norm for conservatives and radicals alike. By this is meant a party which conceives itself as based on dues-paying members, who have rights and duties greater than those of the voters and in particular the right to choose candidates and take part in discussions on policy and organisation. The generalisation holds that these rights are less strongly emphasised in the more conservative parties. But, as R. T. Mackenzie has stressed for Britain, the major parties in bi-partisan systems are becoming increasingly similar in the rights which are extended to individual members. Party discipline tends to be more rigidly applied in the more radical parties, both in parliament and among the enrolled membership. Not only may parliamentarians lose their official endorsement for voting against the party too often, but ordinary rank and file members may be expelled for deviating from policy directives in public, or for working against the party at elections. These practices are accepted by all social-democratic, labour and communist parties in advanced countries, and, less rigidly, by most conservative and liberal parties as well.

The integrated mass party

The fundamental difference between this kind of party and that found in North America, in rural France and in some underdeveloped countries, is that the mass party is conceived of as a brotherhood of the select, while the more loosely structured parties are simply congeries of election committees and fund raisers with no prescriptive rights to direct policy or select candidates. In actual operation there may not be much real difference between parties in Britain and the United States at the local level. The same proportions of voters, usually between five and ten per cent, will be actively associated with the party organisation. The real control of campaigns and candidate selection may rest with an inner-core of semi-professional machine men who rely on loyal supporters. In return these supporters may be allowed some say in the conduct of the campaign. The important difference remains that the selection and policy-making function in British and most European parties is formalised and exclusive to enrolled members, while in the United States it is more informal and depends on expectation of patronage and advancement, rather than on the payment of a regular subscription. Again, as Michels and others have pointed out, the formal policy-making rights of party members in the mass organisation are often illusory and their power to choose candidates may be subject to a great deal of central direction and nomination. However, the mass integrated party depends much less on private donations and local and personal loyalty than is true in North America. It has a far more coherent, because centrally inspired, policy, and one which its active members subscribe to in the belief that they have some say in its formulation. The mass party is thus a more attractive instrument for enforcing radical policies through the electoral process and has been more enthusiastically adopted by radicals. This very adoption, however, forces the conservatives to follow and even surpass in the effectiveness of their organisation.

The potentially totalitarian party

At one extreme, the integrated mass party merges into the party of notables or the loose associational party. At the other it approximates to the potentially totalitarian mode. The dividing line between socialist and communist parties in a competitive situation, in terms of structure and discipline, may sometimes be blurred, just as it is ideologically. However, the communist model, following Lenin's prescription in *What is to be Done?*, tries to articulate itself to social institutions in a fundamentally different way from other parties. It may, in some respects, approximate more to a fascist type of organisation than to a social-democratic. Thus it will tend to favour a military style of discipline, will insist on party control over the

42

politicians, will indoctrinate its membership as a basic activity, will have rules for admission and expulsion much stricter than those of other parties, and will aim at securing power in institutions other than parliament. Communist parties have concentrated much attention on capturing trade union positions, and with great success. They see the union movement as a necessary instrument in politics, which many constitutional parties do not acknowledge. In contrast to social-democrats, who try to differentiate between the functions of unions and the party, communists see the party as dominant and the unions, unemployed associations, housewives leagues and peace groups as instruments. The fundamental difference between potentially totalitarian and other mass parties is that the former have a much wider definition of what constitutes a political institution. When in power, of course, this definition is even expanded and the totalitarian party becomes articulated on a quite different basis from that of constitutional parties in a democratic situation.

National-front organisations

These four types of party, the 'notable led', the loose associational, the integrated mass and the potentially totalitarian, are those most commonly found in competitive situations and in advanced industrial countries. They have served as models for most other parties throughout the world. There are three other types of organisation found mainly in non-competitive situations and largely in the underdeveloped world. These are the national front, the established totalitarian and the guerilla party. All have already established one-party rule or aim at it. The national front is that method of organisation found most commonly in broad and narrow one-party states. It aims at recruiting large sections of the population, while most other types of party are confined to small minorities. Thus the

43

average proportion of adults enrolled in established totalitarian parties is about 8%, and in mass constitutional parties about 12%. But the Democratic Party of Guinea included nearly 70% of adults until November 1964 when some restrictions on admission were introduced. The Tanzanian African National Union includes 60% of Tanzanian adults, while Egypt's Arab Socialist Union has about 33%. In Yugoslavia, Burma and Tunisia, similar proportions are found. The characteristic of national fronts is that they are not restrictive and exclusive like the communists and the nazis, but rather that they embrace all the union, youth, women's and parents' groups which truly totalitarian parties control but do not admit into the party itself. While the membership figures for national fronts may be almost meaningless, they have obviously abandoned the élitist approach of Lenin, who argued 'better fewer, but better'. They are parties of national integration, in wanting everyone to be politically identified with the government. They thus have some function in nations like Yugoslavia or Burma where there are important ethnic differences. However, in contrast to the constitutional mass parties, they rarely offer even nominal powers of policy decision to their members. Because they are essentially governing parties and could not function otherwise, policies are made within the government and transmitted to the mass front.

The established totalitarian party

The established totalitarian party is much more exclusive. Membership is a privilege to be bestowed grudgingly and taken away with alacrity. Because the totalitarian party offers almost the only avenue to promotion in all fields, it can use its rigid discipline to ensure the loyalty of all élites. Thus, in contrast to the potentially totalitarian party, which is articulated towards potentially revolutionary elements, the established totalitarian party is articulated on the established institutions. For example, the Communist Party of the Soviet Union has nearly thirty

44

sections of its Central Committee staffed by full-time officials and their subordinates. Only one-third are concerned with the normal functions of all parties, like organisation, party funds, propaganda and agitation. The rest are responsible for the armed forces, the economy and agriculture, control over ministries, foreign relations, building and construction, and other economic and government functions. These sections, through their subordinate officials, check on all government activity. Party officials normally stand over and above managers, collective farm chairmen, military officers and government officials at the appropriate level. This is not achieved without friction and frequent modification. But essentially the totalitarian party in power is not concerned only with work among the people; it is also the principal means of attaining ideological ends by detailed control. In return its policy-making bodies do tend to consist of those making policy in all other fields. One-fifth of members of the Central Committee of the Soviet Communist Party in 1961 were military officers, while most of the others were government or party officials. The trade union element, so important in potentially totalitarian communist parties, was almost unrepresented.

The guerilla party

The final type of party is one which has emerged in recent years and which is also potentially totalitarian. However, it does not derive from the mass party tradition of Western Europe, as do most communist and fascist parties. This is the 'guerilla party', of which the archetype is the Chinese Communist Party. The guerilla party is one which combines civilian work with military activity and sees the two as complementary and inseparable. In South Vietnam, Bolivia, Peru, Aden, Venezuela, Angola, Congo, Cameroons and Laos, guerilla parties play a major role in politics, as they did previously in Malaya and the Philippines. In China, Cuba, Yugoslavia, Algeria and North Vietnam guerilla parties have achieved power, becoming totalitarian in doing so, but retaining features which the 'civilian' communist parties have either lost or never possessed. Among these is a tendency to glorify the partisans and even to place them above the civilian party. In China the People's Liberation Army is obviously in that position at present with the civilian, conventional communists typified by Liu Shao-chi in disgrace. The guerilla party is distinct from the military junta type of party in that it creates the military leaders and is not created by them. It is articulated along military lines rather than simply being a civilian party with a militarised or subversive wing, as the Indian and Indonesian Communists temporarily became in 1948. Typically the guerilla party operates in states with very low urbanisation, with political institutions which are not fully legitimised because of incompetence or foreign origins, with traditions of popular brigandage often based on mountain regions and accessibility to arms resulting from postwar conditions or the corruptibility of the armed forces. The guerilla party grows by taking over areas, raising taxes and conscripts within them and administering them in accordance with party principles. Today most such parties are communist and support Peking rather than Moscow. However, this is not necessarily the only ideology giving rise to guerilla parties. Anarchism, nationalism or populism have been important drives in the past, especially in the Latin and Slav countries. Nor need a guerilla party necessarily create a totalitarian system if victorious. In Eire, it could be argued, Fianna Fail has essentially guerilla origins in the Irish Republican Army, but has long ago settled down to parliamentary politics. In Mexico and Yugoslavia systems have grown out of guerilla conditions which are some way from the classic totalitarian model.

The guerilla party exists at the point where the organisational typology of parties ends and that of movements

46

begins. There is little agreement among political scientists on the boundary between parties and movements. This is not surprising as a large proportion of parties had their origins in movements and may retain some of the terminology and attitudes of the movement long after they became clearly political parties. In popular parlance, people talk not only of the socialist, labour or communist movements, but also of the conservative movement, whatever that may be. The only common factor in this use of the term is the suggestion that parties are something less than a brotherhood of dedicated ideologies, that somehow they are are engaged in 'politics', whereas the movement is striving after 'ideals'. Most definitions of movements stress that they are based on deep ideological commitment but the same could be said of many parties. If a definition is needed, it might be fruitful to describe movements as oriented towards the achieving of goals, rather than the capture of power. Their organisation may thus be informal and unstructured. It need not be articulated on the existing government institutions because the movement may aim at their overthrow or simply at pressure on those already in office without their replacement. Thus it makes sense to talk of the trade union movement, the peace movement, the civil rights movement, nationalist movements, where all of these are organised for winning mass support but not for winning direct political power through elections or revolutions. The organisational form most appropriate to movements is one centred on propaganda, whereas that most appropriate to a party is one based on capturing power and extending patronage.

The working of organisations

The above attempts to construct an organisational typology useful for distinguishing parties in action. It does not tell us precisely how the structure of a party is operated. For that, detailed study of the party machine over a period

47

of years is necessary. Practices change even while rules remain the same. Rules may be changed but obscure a continuity of practice. Any attempt to distinguish between loose, indistinct parties, integrated mass parties and ideologically committed totalitarian parties, must make certain assumptions. It is very difficult to measure the degree of commitment to programmes and ideas of a party as a whole, without detailed questioning. Most surveys in modern societies show that whereas there is a great deal of disagreement between the activists of different parties, there is a major overlap of attitudes between the passive members and voters. There is also wide consensus between practising politicians in office, where their main source of information is the public service or economic interest groups rather than the party. Even such ideologically committed parties as the French or Italian Communists have to acknowledge that their voters, trade union adherents and members are not ideologically pure by any means and may be more strongly influenced by religious or nationalist fervours than by the atheistic internationalism of the official party line. Thus, when it is argued that there is a difference in kind between American and European parties in terms of their commitment to an ideology, this must be accepted as only another way of saying that a line has been drawn beyond which a difference of degree is taken as a difference in kind. The same is true of any division between radical mass movements and potentially totalitarian parties. Where the difference in kind is measurable is when the totalitarian party wins power and transforms itself into a directive party quite different from its original self, if ostensibly based on a common tradition.

The other important distinguishing mark between different types of party is the degree of discipline and internal cohesion. The complicating factor here is that factionalism is endemic to party politics, no matter what the rules say. It may be consistently suppressed, as in

48

Communism, or institutionalised, as in the United States. It breaks out nevertheless, confusing the simple picture. Factionalism is easier the more a party approximates to the 'notable' model and away from the 'totalitarian' model. The intensity and frequency of factionalism has to be taken into account when deciding on the basic features of any particular party. Thus, despite formal acceptance of a rigid Leninist model, the Indian Communist Party has always been faction-ridden and conducts its disagreements in public. British Communists are much more circumspect, the French are more rigidly disciplined than the Italians, and so on. Thus, within the category of 'potentially totalitarian' it is possible to discern differences of degree which may tell us something of the likely consequences of any particular party gaining office.

Factionalism can be affected by the kind of political system to which the party organisation is articulated. Thus the Australian Labour Party, in a federal system, has been much more openly and disastrously factional than the British, despite a more authoritarian attitude to party discipline. Federalism especially encourages factionalism, as the United States, Canada and India all show. The national leaders are dependent on provincial leaders who bargain with them and with each other in a situation of constant compromise and coalition which is much less common in a unitary system like the British. The social features of a country also influence factionalism, by giving it a base. Thus in a one-party system like Yugoslavia, the old rivalries between Serbs, Croats, Slovenes and Macedonians are now being played out within a quasi-federal political system and within the Yugoslav League of Communists itself. A party which is organised on what Duverger has called 'indirect structure', that is with affiliated organisations not completely under party control, has an inducement to factionalism built into it. Most such parties have functioned in socially homogeneous and unitary systems like those of Britain and Scandinavia and have thus been spared too much disruption. However, even the social-democratic 'indirectly structured' parties of those states have known tensions between the industrial and political wings.

The degree of factionalism and of programmatic or ideological commitment must be studied together with the formal rules of the party in order to categorise it accurately. As Mackenzie has shown, the realities of policy making and leadership selection must be analysed alongside the party's myths and forms. For parties are not simply 'models'. They are forms of collective action within which sociological and social psychological forces are at work. These are constrained by the party structure but not completely suppressed by it.

4

Parties in modernised societies

The longest established party systems are found in modernised societies. Such societies have a high level of urbanisation and industrialisation, universal literacy, a high national income per head, largely derived from industry and commerce, and, in most cases, competitive parliamentary institutions based on universal suffrage and fully established for at least twenty-five years. There are some partly modernised societies like South Africa, with its large African population excluded from party politics, Japan with a major traditionalist rural sector, and Israel with its massive immigration from backward Jewish communities in Africa and the Middle East. There are also systems like those of France or Argentina where restrictions are placed on parliament and where states of emergency have occurred in recent years. On the whole, however modernised societies are the most politically stable. This seems to be nearly as true for the three totalitarian modern societies of the Soviet Union, East Germany and Czechoslovakia, as for the democracies of Europe, North America and Australasia. However, because of their fundamentally different political systems, these three states will be considered in Chapter 6.

About one-sixth of all party systems, or just over twenty, are both modernised and competitive. They cover a population of nearly six hundred and fifty million people. With a few exceptions, of which the United States is the most outstanding, these party systems are based on hierarchically structured and coherent mass parties, one or more of which normally have organisational links with a strong trade union movement. In fact the United States, Uruguay and South Africa are the only modernised societies in which there is no significant socialist, communist or syndicalist movement; in Canada and Switzerland parties in this broad category normally poll less than 30% of the total vote. Thus the mass working-class party is a significant factor in the political system of most modernised societies, as are competitive elections and stable parties. There are three broad types of politics and different party features. These may be termed the 'American', 'European' and the 'Anglo-Scandinavian' for convenience. These three correspond to the categories of *indistinct bi-partisan*, *multi-party* and *distinct bi-partisan* respectively. Some nations fit uncomfortably into these, for example Japan, where the divisions between the distinctive parties are more acute than in the 'Anglo-Scandinavian' bracket. West Germany, however, fits this group much more easily than in the past, when it might more reasonably have been classed with the 'European' states like France, Italy, Belgium or Holland.

Different styles of politics characterise these systems. In the United States, Uruguay and most of Canada, historic parties of early or mid-nineteenth century origin have been undisturbed. Many of their practices, and their characteristic domination by the professional and business classes, reflect this heritage from the past. The Republicans and Democrats, the Conservatives and Liberals, the Blancos and Colorados, have been able to cope with mass immigration, industrialisation and substantial social rearrangement by being loosely structured and indisciplined, ideologically vague and thus resistant to schism. Even the severe social strains caused by Negro and French-Canadian resentments have been largely accommodated within the

52

existing parties. Farmer-labour, social credit, populist and even socialist movements have arisen. They, too, are either incorporated within the existing parties or, as in Canada, are confined to certain regions of the country. This is an adjustive and absorptive style of politics in which strains which would destroy more rigid and committed parties are simply adapted to. The price which has had to be paid is a lagging behind Europe in social welfare programmes, the protection of trade unionism and the care of the poor and of minorities. There is a characteristic failure to understand or sympathise with the socialist movements which flourish in the rest of the world. However, on the credit side, the party system does not restrict discussion to ideologically sanctioned approaches, it does not impose rigidities and it is capable of recruiting political leaders from a wide range of talents. The American system, by its wide use of the electoral process, opens more choices to the general population than do the exclusive European mass parties. Positions as delegates and candidates, whose choice is confined to subscribing members in Europe, are subject to popular election by party supporters in the U.S.A. This completely blurs the distinction between 'member' and 'voter' which is vital to hierarchically organised mass parties. This is an important factor in the failure of American parties to adhere to distinctive programmes.

The 'European' style of politics is essentially fragmented. Social strains produce new movements. Religious and social schisms are not accommodated within amorphous parties but are mirrored in the multi-party system. Most nations in the 'European' category have suffered from revolutionary violence between classes and groups and some have experienced years of dictatorship. The contrast with New World politics is immediate. Despite violence, authoritarianism and sectional strife in the United States and Canada, leading to civil war in both in the middle of last century, competitive democracy and the amorphous parties have survived. 'European' politics has been less capable of dealing with strains. Ideological movements have nearly all originated in central Europe and spread their ideas throughout the world. Religious schism is as important in this process as social or cultural tension. The class struggle was not necessarily more acute in Germany than in the United States. Other struggles, for the franchise, against the Catholic Church, for and against the authority of the state, make the European situation more combustible and less capable of resolution than the American. To argue that European countries are somehow less effectively modernised than the North American, is very difficult to sustain. Traditionalism and rural backwardness are just as apparent in Mississippi or Nova Scotia as in Franconia. The vital difference is that European politics has had to absorb the struggle against conservative institutions which were left behind by emigrants to the New World.

The 'Anglo-Scandinavian' systems, to which West Germany and Austria have moved from their previous 'European' position, are distinct from the others, although related to them. Like the European, they have given rise to mass parties, and especially to union-based labour parties. Like the Americans they have largely avoided fragmented parties, preferring the broad coalition within which various interests compete. To a great extent this has been because the 'Anglo-Scandinavian' states of Britain, Sweden, Norway, Denmark, Australia and New Zealand, have been culturally homogeneous. Social-democracy has flourished because its appeal to the working classes has not been confused by sectarian or linguistic resentments. In Australia, the only one of these states with less than 85% of its people in Protestant denominations, the labour movement has been severely split along religious lines and has become politically ineffective in recent years. These states could just as meaningfully be categorised as 'social-democratic'. Even the conservative parties have accepted the consumer style of politics, with the state providing many of the benefits, regulating the economy and ameliorating conditions likely to produce social strain. The essential feature of these systems is the calmness of politics coupled with the general acceptance of state intervention. Political alignments are still based largely on social class but class consciousness is not highly developed except at the extremes of unskilled manual and higher professional and business occupations. Voting across classes is very common and without it conservative parties could scarcely survive in most modern societies.

The decline of party strife?

A marked feature of all but the still modernising industrial societies has been the blurring of distinctions between parties in terms of voting support and ideology. In North America the lines were never as clearly drawn as in Europe and discussion of 'the end of ideology' is thus unsatisfactory in that context. Even in Europe there has never been the clear cut difference between the broad 'Anglo-Scandinavian' parties or some of the 'European' centre parties, which exists at the Left and Right extremes. Despite the intangibility of concepts like 'convergence on the centre' it is clear, however, that the tensions of political life are less than in the past. The active interest of the voters has declined and many battles are now over. In West Germany and Austria the once Marxist social-democrats have gone into coalition with parties whose predecessors suppressed and exterminated socialists within living memory. In every country of the European Common Market, socialist and Catholic parties have acted together in coalition at some time in the past fifteen years. These arrangements have usually been quite harmonious except on the one issue of state aid for religious education. In Britain, where peacetime coalitions have not appeared, there was three-party agreement in 1967 on the need to enter the Common Market and to change all Britain's traditional links. The temper of politics in Scandinavia and Australasia has become very cool. Parties enjoy many years in office (35 in Sweden, 21 in Norway and 18 in Australia), suggesting general satisfaction with policies which are broadly accepted by all major parties.

Bi-partisan foreign policies are now common throughout the modernised countries, except for Japan. Bi-partisan acceptance of the welfare state, of the maintenance of full employment, of manipulated economies, is also very common. Moreover, parties are no longer as clearly tied to their supporting interests as they once were. Most social-democratic parties now have professional middle-class parliamentarians, rather than trade unionists and manual workers. In Holland the trade unions have already severed their formal connection with the Labour Party. The German Christian Democratic Party is not specifically Catholic, as its Centre Party predecessor was, but appeals to Protestants and, by its social welfare and worker management policies, to industrial workers as well. There are clear signs that the 'Anglo-Scandinavian' states are following the North American in the tendency for voters to become detached from loyalty to one party only. Wild swings in electoral support are becoming common, suggesting that class appeals are no longer enough to secure allegiance. These swings move in either direction and are not, as some were arguing in Britain in 1959, consistently against the labour and socialist parties. Class is no longer clearly defined in terms of life style or expectations, though occupational stratification is still important. In particular there is now a long-term trend in all completely industrialised countries for the manual occupations to decline and for service and 'white collar' jobs to increase. This is reflected in stagnant or even declining trade union recruitment.

Along with this blurring of distinctions which were

fairly clear-cut twenty or thirty years ago, has gone a tendency to reduce the importance of the parties in decision and policy making. Already in the United States and Canada the parties as a whole were not very concerned with this role, but left it to individual leaders or groups of politicians. Party control was exercised through patronage and the national leader. In Europe, however, most parties saw themselves as at the centre of political goal attainment. The ideological movements carried this to extremes but more pragmatic parties were also committed to consciously shaping national ends. This role has been reduced in a number of ways. In France, where party structure was very fluid, ideological extremes well represented and coalition endemic, General de Gaulle has deliberately limited the functions of partisans under the constitution of the Fifth Republic. Ministers are appointed by the President from civil servants and Parliament has limited control over them. In May 1967 the General introduced emergency powers for six months to expedite economic reforms. Although challenged by the trade unions, this effectively pushed the parties out of the centre of national policy making altogether. De Gaulle's own party is a very loosely structured and ideologically vague amalgam of previously conservative factions which he refuses to join.

In the rest of Europe the reduction of partisan influence stems from the creation of coalitions in which the separate parties have to sink their differences. Austria enjoyed a unique bi-partisan coalition for nearly twenty years, while West Germany has just adopted one. In Italy, the 'centre-Left' arrangement brings together previously hostile parties, leaving the Communist and fascist extremes in isolation. Even more important than this submersion by coalition, has been the transfer of some functions in the European Common Market to the European Commission at Brussels. While many of the professional bureaucrats in the Commission have previously held government office, they are not primarily partisan and are expected to sever themselves from purely national loyalties. This is perhaps the most extreme example of a trend apparent throughout the modernised systems. Party is becoming increasingly specialised and limited in its role. From being a secular religion, integrating its members into a complete social and intellectual life, the European mass party is becoming limited to electioneering and the selection of candidates. Membership is declining in most parties. Where it is not, the intensity of commitment seems to be fading, with meetings held less frequently, rallies sparsely attended, and youth movements dying. These trends are not as strong everywhere. For example, the organisation of the Swedish and Austrian socialists or the Italian Communists have retained effectiveness and virility. In general most parties seem slowly to be losing their distinctive nature as collectivities of the committed, and to be approximating to the North American pattern of the election machine.

This specialisation of party functions parallels a decline in the notion of the party as the controlling force in social and political change. Trade union organisations, while mostly still linked to mass parties, are reducing their political involvement and specialising as pressure groups in direct relationships with the government bureaucracy. Business corporations, while still subscribing to conservative parties, have learnt to live with socialist governments and have even provided some of the personnel of public corporations and government departments. The universities, while still a centre of ideological debate and of recruitment into party politics, are equally providing their knowledge direct to government, by-passing the political parties unless frustrated by bureaucratic indifference to professional help. All of these trends tend to sap the vitality of the parties and reduce their role in national policy making. As government bureaucracies expand and become more efficient, and as the same happens to other private bureaucracies, so the parties find it increasingly difficult to keep up with the supply of specifically partisan information. Their parliamentarians look increasingly to non-partisan agencies for their information. This, together with the general lowering of social tensions which affluence brings, steadily drains the content from ideological or even programmatic differences. Every issue comes to be solved by debate between professional experts. The party leaders join in, and usually retain the power of final decision. In making such decision they are less likely to refer to the party machines and to partisan programmes and ideologies.

As the party becomes more specialised as a purely vote-getting and élite selection agency, so the reasons for maintaining discipline and mass enthusiasm begin to wither. Even party propaganda passes into the hands of advertising agents, not simply in North America but also in Britain, Australasia and, for the first time in 1967, in France. The very techniques of electioneering change as public interest shifts from meetings, pamphlets and newspapers to television. It is characteristic of all modernised societies, except currently South Africa, that there is high or almost complete penetration by all mass media. The world's highest proportions of newspaper readership and television ownership are all in Britain, Scandinavia, Japan, Australasia and North America. The elector's total reliance on the mass media makes professional approaches more important and amateur enthusiasms apparently useless. Meetings are only held to attract mass media coverage. Party stalwarts wear rosettes and collect membership dues. Party officials are wondering whether this is still necessary. In North America and increasingly in Europe, parties depend on donations from corporations and pressure groups rather than small sums from a mass membership. The main task of the rank and file is thus limited to combatting the apathy of the electors by cajoling them into turning out on election day. Even this is often accomplished by paid canvassers, where election expense regulations allow it. The volunteer feels increasingly isolated not only from policy making, but also from any essential role in the functioning of the party.

Reactions against futility

The party systems of modernised societies are mostly permanent. They rest on institutions which have lasted through more than one generation. Thus in the mass parties there are still many who work from habit, or from an inadequate perception of the power relations within their organisation. Where the parties retain some vestige of ideology the membership is sustained by the appeal of knowing the truth. Like members of religious denominations, they do not question the value of what they are doing. Thus the tendency towards bureaucratic and technocratic usurpation of party functions outlined above has not yet seriously eroded the major parties, though some have lost one half or more of their formally enrolled members in the past twenty years. Moreover there are waves of enthusiasm, when major changes are expected. These draw new people into partisan activity and reactivate those who have fallen out. Recruitment from the young is still possible although certainly not as easy as in the past. Thus the mass parties are not likely to degenerate to a loose association of election committees, losing all other function and giving up any pretence at policy formulation. They attempt, by themselves employing specialists, to act as a counterweight to the bureaucracy. The resources which the British Labour Party can call up from the universities, the unions and the professions are still substantial and may, in some fields, be more competent than the relatively small group of decision makers in the higher civil service. The parties themselves become much more professionalised. This is equally true for the United States, as the Kennedy era most firmly

60

underlined. Even where the party as a whole is not programmatic, individual politicians employ considerable staffs for briefing and publicity. The American system of patronage makes it easy to move partisans into bureaucratic posts and this is true to some extent for Europe, and has even been marginally attempted by the Wilson Labour government in Britain. Thus it is not the party which is dying, but rather the party's function as a secular religion, as a party of integration, as a transmission belt between the politically interested and the government. For the very professionalisation of the party which helps preserve it, also helps to drive the inexpert rank and file further from the centre of power.

In all modern societies there are far more politically involved people than are found in the bureaucracies of government and party. Previously these had an outlet in the struggle over ideologies. Many are still satisfied with the politics of affluence, playing it like a football supporters' club in terms of winning or losing a game. This sentiment is probably strong enough in itself to guarantee the survival of parties, as long as there are any social differences to speak of, and as long as competitive elections force candidates into differing programmatic positions. This kind of incentive to active support is not satisfying to those who saw the parties as secular religions. They will remain doggedly with ideological movements, as millions of Frenchmen and Italians have done, or will search around for substitutes for the converging and bureaucratised parties. Thus a reaction against the consumer approach to politics sets in. The bargaining for votes among a satisfied affluent electorate becomes unattractive and calls go out for a return to fundamentals. These reflect psychological needs as much as sectional demands. Very often the 'new ideologues' want to do things for people who seem unable to do them for themselves or are considered too apathetic and spoiled by prosperity to become interested in politics.

The 'revolt of youth' which has been so widely commented on throughout the modern world, is one example of this frustration. It does not always take political form but where it does is formidable, if ephemeral. The Campaign for Nuclear Disarmament, the Civil Rights Movement, the Dutch 'provos', the Japanese Zengakuren, are all important examples of this trend. They flourished outside the formal party structure, but in relationship with it. Most of the leaders were disappointed by consumer politics and wanted ideals injected into what had become for them a dull and meaningless game. The form of action was characteristic of a movement rather than a party. Rallies, marches, theatrical displays and occasional violence all shocked the established parties. They gave an outlet to young people who could get no satisfaction from the marginal adjustments which interested their elders. Another form of frustration which the parties have not been able to resolve has been that of ethnic minorities who feel ignored in majority-based competitive politics. The Black Muslim movement, the French-Canadians, the Tyroleans, the Walloons, even the Welsh and the Scots, find it hard to accept the major established parties as standing for their interests. They form movements and parties of their own, which challenge the purely economic appeals of consumer politics by introducing cultural complaints. These attract into movements those who are not consoled by the major parties.

These three bases for revolt, the youth, minorities and the spiritually starved, are more capable of forming transitory movements than permanent parties. By acting through parties they may produce startling results, as the New Right did in the Republican Party or the Campaign for Nuclear Disarmament in British Labour. There is little real evidence that they can coalesce into a stable enough movement to emulate the ideologues of the past. What they do is to divert from conventional parties the activists and even the voters who cannot be satisfied by economic

concessions and expertly engineered adjustments to existing arrangements. Without such revolts, party politics in
modernised societies would become even more bi-partisan
and professionalised, fulfilling highly specialised electoral
functions and little else.

5

Mass radicalism

A distinctive type of party grew up in the late nineteenth century because classes and nations began to respond to radical appeals. While both socialism and nationalism were brought to the repressed classes and nations by bourgeois or cosmopolitan intellectuals, they grew into important movements because the response could be aroused, the party formed and the masses brought into politics. Where socialism did not appeal, as in the United States, or nationalism found a hollow echo, as in Scotland or Wales, then the parties and movements which were formed simply stagnated or withered. Nonetheless, mass radicalism was a feature of European politics between 1870 and 1945 and has spread to Asia and to parts of Latin America, the Middle East and Africa in more recent times.

The mass radical party often began as a movement. Its adherents were excluded from the political process and organised themselves in order to force inclusion. Movements are distinguished from parties by their commitment to an ideology, their mobilisation of enthusiasm and their scorn for established political institutions and practices. The radical movements of the nineteenth century had all of these characteristics and have passed them on to their successors, the radical parties. Because those to whom they appealed were outside the controlling

64

élite, the mass movement used different methods from those of the established rulers. Some movements, most notably the Populists of Tsarist Russia, denied the validity of all existing forms of authority, while others simply looked for the extension of embryonic liberalism until it granted universal suffrage or the liberation of oppressed nations. The nineteenth-century movement was fairly loosely organised but this need not be characteristic of modern movements. Parties, too, were much less disciplined and coherent than today and the illegality of many mass movements made them operate in such a way that no central organisation could be discovered and destroyed. The Chartists in Britain, the Populists in Russia, and the national movements of Italy and the Balkans, were all decentralised, indisciplined and ideologically vague by modern standards.

The movements grew into parties once they were given the opportunity to gain some access to power. The Chartists, although dying by 1850, exerted some influence on radicalism and trade unionism until their ideas became one inspiration for the British Labour Party. The Russian Populists, repressed into fragmented anarchism by 1885, passed on their heritage to the Social Revolutionary Party, founded in 1902 and still the only Russian party to win a competitive election. The union and co-operative movement in Germany, influenced by Lassalle, gave rise to the Social Democratic Party, which was the model for all European socialist parties until 1914. The Indian National Congress, a loosely organised and essentially élitist movement formed in 1885, reorganised itself as a mass party after 1921 with expanding opportunities for Indian participation in collective political decisions. The common feature of all these movements, as of the Kuomintang and Communist Party of China, was that they operated for many years outside the established ruling classes and against them, recruited mass membership when the élite party of 'notables' was the standard form of their societies, and formalised themselves into effective, permanent mass parties once their propaganda had been accepted by crucial segments of their publics.

These movement-created parties were models for other parties until large areas of the world became influenced by mass radicalism. European socialism spread into Russia and the Balkans where it combined with populism into communism. This in turn spread into Asia and back into Europe in competition with its socialist inspirers. Another strain of populism produced the peasant parties of Eastern Europe while yet another influenced the thinking of Gandhi and a wing of the Indian National Congress. Anarchist notions spread from Spain to Latin America where, as in Italy, anarcho-syndicalism became a basis for both communism and fascism, while retaining some of its own strength. Socialism, populism and communism had become intermingled by the 1920's and there were no developed systems which were not influenced by them. The syndicalist Industrial Workers of the World organised among immigrant workers in the United States, overlapped with native American populism, with the then powerful American Socialist Party and with those who were to found the American Communist Party. The prosperity and repression of the 1920's killed the prospect of mass radicalism breaking through the established party system as it was doing in Britain at the same time. The U.S.A. and, to a lesser extent, Canada, remained isolated and immune. Other parts of the Americas were not. Powerful parties have grown in Mexico, Peru and Argentina on the basis of socialist and syndicalist ideas and mass organisation.

Mass radicalism took many forms and the parties which arose from it are now varied and often extremely hostile to each other. The prosperous and stable democracies of North-western Europe and Australasia created union-based labour parties with mild Marxist or populist overtones. Germany and Austria built powerful social-democratic parties which were suppressed by fascism but have revived and remain central to their politics. In an important sense fascism in Italy and Nazism in Germany combined traditionalist attitudes with mass radical slogans and techniques. Above all communism, with its control over one-third of the world, carried mass radicalism to its totalitarian conclusion. Nationalist movements have incorporated attitudes from the radical tradition. The Indian National Congress has been eclectic enough to incorporate the populism of Gandhi, the liberal socialism of Kripalani, Nehru and Mehta, and the fascism of Bhose, the conservatism of Patel, official Stalinism and traditional Hinduism. Other national movements have been less inclusive. Nationalism has, however, moved away from the liberal philosophy and élite leadership typical of the nineteenth century. The Convention Peoples Party of Ghana, the Democratic Party of Senegal, the Partai Nasional Indonesia, all show clearly their mass radical inspiration.

The socialist parties

The first movements to become institutionalised into parties were the European socialists. The German Social-Democratic Party was formed in 1874 and remained at the centre of European socialism until 1914. It was not approved of by Marx, nor by Bismarck, who made it illegal. With its legalisation in 1891 and the adoption of a Marxist programme at its Erfurt congress, the party was able to build its organisation and electoral following. It was rivalled in success only by the Austrian party. A class of party organisers, politicians and editors grew up and mass membership of predominantly working class character made social democracy by far the best organised movement in Europe before 1914. It also showed quite clearly the dilemmas which were to beset social-democracy. The analyses of Bernstein and Rosa Luxemburg, the academic dissection of Michels and Weber, the

67

increasingly arid glosses on Marxism produced by Bebel and Kautsky, all show the difficulties of turning a movement into a constitutional mass party. A movement is free, irresponsible and dynamic. An established party is inhibited, comprising and bureaucratic. Nowhere was this truer than in Imperial Germany. Despite manhood suffrage, large areas of national policy were not controlled by the legislature. The party had been illegal for many years and was never accepted as legitimate by the social, military and business élites. Moreover it was so highly organised, and so many personal livelihoods were tied up with its preservation, that it could take no risks.

German social-democracy claimed to be Marxist, revolutionary, internally democratic and internationalist. These were the myths which bound its vast membership together and attracted increasing proportions of the electorate. As a movement shifts from agitation to electioneering, however, it must come to grips with its public on a new level. Votes are more difficult to gain than cheers and more depends on them. The party's success in a competitive system is judged not by the purity of its ideology or the elaborateness of its organisation. Seats won and votes gained are the only concrete and irrefutible measures which exist in electoral politics. As the party moves further out towards the limits of its loyal support, so its movement characteristics become more of an embarrassment. The Marxist scheme, with its echoes of the revolutions of 1848, was increasingly untenable. Only Bernstein had the courage to point out publicly that misery was not increasing, that the State could be used as a neutral instrument for social progress, that the German workers were not revolutionary and were never likely to be, and that support would be attracted by an ethical appeal, not because it was inevitable. There is very little in what Bernstein said in *Evolutionary Socialism* sixty years ago which was not still being said by Gaitskell, Crosland and their European fellow 'revisionists' in more recent years. All socialist parties operating in a competitive milieu have had to rationalise the passage from movement to party at some time in this century.

On the other wing of the party were those who wanted it to remain a movement. With some justification, as events in the 1930's showed, Luxemburg and Liebknecht argued, and Lenin was to echo, that the State within which the party operated was controlled by those who were hostile to social-democracy and that it could not be captured by a simple majority of the electors. Those who favoured the retention of movement militancy were better prophets for central Europe than was Bernstein. But sociologically he was quite correct when he wrote that 'the movement is everything, the aim nothing'. German social-democracy had become an end in itself, as all established mass parties do. Michels showed that its claims to an internal democracy were not tenable, that 'socialists may triumph but socialism never'. All European socialist and labour parties since have proved Michels' point. What begins as a device for eliciting the opinions of the members of the mass movement, becomes hardened into a complicated and cumbersome hierarchy. As in all bureaucracies, protests from below become muted into mild complaints. The leadership, whether in parliament or in the machine, controls the policy-making process if only because it has knowledge denied to the rank and file. No established party can retain intact the methods of the mass movement from which it originates.

The mass labour parties

The British, Scandinavian and Australasian socialist movements have not been faced with quite the same problems as mainstream European socialism. While the Norwegian party was subject to schisms in trying to retain Marxist purity while working competitive politics, this group of parties arose essentially from the trade unions. Unions, despite their movement origins, very quickly became institutionalised. In the past thirty years they have been increasingly wedded to the administrative machine as governments have realised the effect of wage claims on the national economy rather than on the individual employer. On the whole the union official in a stable society has a limited political view. He is not susceptible to messianic visions nor very willing to test the strength of his organisation in revolutionary adventures. Even more than the mass party, the union is bureaucratised, conserves its energies and funds, limits its vision to immediate goals and channels the energies and resentments of its members into controlled campaigns. The unions in those democracies with mass labour parties have been united and not subject to those schisms found in Europe and South Asia. The societies on which they are based are racially, culturally and religiously fairly homogeneous and there are no important rivals to distract loyalty from the party which most manual unions support. With the exception of Australia, the unions have been a conservative force in mass labour parties.

Despite all this, the painful transformation from movement into party has not been avoided altogether by the labour parties. Each party contains an element which is more in sympathy with traditional socialism than are the majority of the party's supporters and most of its elected politicians. This element may be the 'conscience' of the party, helping it to retain its distinctiveness from conservative rivals. A socialist element is also useful in running campaigns on issues which the party is unable or unwilling to take up because of its innate caution. This was the major function of the 'Unity Campaigns' in Britain in the 1930's. The Labour Party was very reluctant to support unemployed marches banned by the Trades Union Congress, to fight Mosley's fascists in the streets of London or to organise mass meetings for the Spanish

70

republicans or against appeasement of Hitler. The Left Wing of the party, which overlapped with the Communists, was able to do all these things. At the time Labour was embarrassed and hostile, fearing the electoral consequences. In the changed atmosphere after the Second World War, however, the actions of the pre-War Left became part of the official Labour mythology. Like Bernstein, the sociologically perceptive leaders of labour parties find it hard to revert to the tactics of the original movement even when protest is called for. It is then that the old-fashioned and backward looking radicals come into their own and fulfil a useful function.

Apart from re-orienting itself to mundane tasks, the labour party shows tensions between its 'industrial' and its 'political' wings. Most labour parties are based on trade union affiliation or, at the very least, depend heavily upon union funds for survival. This introduces a complication into the party hierarchy. The directly structured socialist parties of Europe worked on the assumption that a two-way process of instruction and command would operate throughout the complicated mass machine. Labour parties add a new dimension by drafting full-time union officials backed by the votes of their organisations, into the decision-making processes. Parties and unions will not necessarily have the same approach nor be interested in the same things. Unions have to deal with conservative governments and may feel that association with a radical opposition will make them less effective. Such fears are rarely held in reverse by businessmen supporting conservative parties, but union officials are often less confident of their importance to the nation. The easiest relationship is that of Sweden, where a labour party has governed for over thirty years and the frictions which have existed with the union movement in the early days of the party have disappeared. In other labour parties there is a constant tension, based often on class resentment. The mass labour party is certainly democratic in its internal processes but it has added yet another divisive force in the affiliated unions, if one which it can often tame.

The labour party is formed by the unions, co-operating with a socialist group of diminutive size but inspirational importance. It is this minority which wants to retain the movement characteristic and is impatient with the conservative leaders and even more conservative voters. For labour parties have normally functioned only in countries which were economically advanced, urbanised and relatively free of major social cleavage. It seems a precondition for the success of mass labour parties that social homogeneity and economic stability form the basis of the society. Where the labour force is fragmented racially or ethnically, as in the United States, where religion plays a major political role as in Italy, or where the economy collapses as in Weimar Germany in 1933, then mass labour or social-democratic parties cannot be expected to flourish.

The communist parties

In the countries of Europe, and later of Asia, where the conditions for successful social-democracy were not fully established, the radical, anti-clerical, labour and reforming movements became susceptible to revolutionary slogans. They turned to syndicalism and then, after 1917, to communism. In those European countries where it flourished, communism was normally the inheritor rather than the initiator, of a mass movement. In Asia, by contrast, and most notably in China and Indonesia, the absence of pre-existing mass radical movements left the initiating role to tiny groups of communists with specifically revolutionary aims. For this, as for many other reasons, one would expect the communist parties of Asia and of Eastern Europe to be less likely to institutionalise themselves as on-going parts of a multi-party constitutional

72

system. The most successful communist movements have grown up in conditions where society was so fragmented and traditional, and where authority was so rigidly imposed, that no non-revolutionary path was open. In those conditions communism remains true to its revolutionary origins until power is seized. Then the party becomes a rigid hierarchy for control over and patronage within, a totalitarian system. In more advanced nations, however, communists face the same dilemma as did the social-democrats. They must become part of the system, or they must remain minor sects with only a pressure-group role which frustrates their ostensible purpose.

The communist movement is much more consciously oriented towards goals and much more uniformly organised than any other mass movement. This makes it very difficult for a party to adjust itself to the process of institutionalisation. Schisms will occur more frequently than in the broad social-democratic movements. In the present Sino-Soviet conflict, in most countries it is the traditional revolutionaries who have veered towards Peking, the bureaucrats, union officials and parliamentarians who have stayed with Moscow. All communist parties outside the one-third of the world in which they have been victorious, are faced with schism and with the prospect of permanent ineffectiveness. Since the decimating of the Indonesian Communist Party in late 1966 there are only five non-ruling communist parties with more than 50,000 members. This, of course, obscures the reality of communist control over unions and front organisations which may be substantial. But the Indonesian experience suggests that this kind of control is not a revolutionary device. It is only effective as long as the mass membership is not driven too far. Similarly, in stable modernised systems like Italy and France, massive communist parties and union movements have been reduced to virtual impotence because they cannot in fact use their mass following any more effectively than can most social-democratic and labour parties. As Lenin observed sixty years ago, the further the communists reach out into the masses, the more likely they are to be swallowed up by them.

Mass radicalism

The formation and maintenance of mass radical movements has been a feature of most advanced states, and especially of those with large populations and considerable cities. Only Mao Tse-Tung has been fully successful in creating and sustaining a mass peasant movement and driving it into power. His methods were, of course, just as much military as political. They rested on the belief that politics and military operations are inseparable. In most other major nations the mass movement has been an urban phenomenon. The Indian Congress, through Gandhi, was able to establish contact with the peasants and to mobilise them for short campaigns. It remained largely under the control of urban intellectuals and merchants and was dependent on Bombay and Calcutta finance. The more typical mass movement is found in an industrial country, often in the earlier stages of industrialisation. Large numbers of country people are being drafted into the cities at the same time as the middle-class radical campaign for suffrage is under way or already completed. The mass radical movement is normally based on the industrial masses, led or inspired to some extent by members of the middle classes who have been excluded from or are alienated from the centres of power. Even the United States went through phases of mass movement, particularly among the Scandinavians and East Europeans who supported both farmer-labour movements and the I.W.W. American industrialisation differed from that of Europe, however, in that its labour force was not homogeneous. This, and the ever-open frontier or the ethic of individual

74

success which went with it, seems a major factor preventing the institutionalisation of mass radicalism in the United States. For if mass action fails to recruit, it must wither or ally itself to the existing political forces.

Elsewhere the generalisation that mass movements are a typical phenomenon of the later stages of industrial revolution generally holds. Deliberate repression, as in Japan or in Bismarck Germany, may hold up a mass movement or turn it into revolutionary channels. Where the franchise is open, as in Australasia, the rise of the movement and its adoption of parliamentary methods will be more rapid than in closed systems. Whatever the background and details one would expect the mass movement to face a number of difficulties along its path. In the American situation it faces the danger of becoming a withering minority, or failing to catch on. Where it does become a permanent feature of the parliamentary scene one would expect constant tensions between leaders wedded to the political system and followers committed to the original aims. Where an unstable revolutionary situation exists, or is created by the movement, then the danger of physical destruction, suffered by German Social Democrats and Indonesian Communists alike, is a very real one. Radical mass movements which retain a purely civilian character are, in fact, very vulnerable to this kind of destruction. They are too cumbersome, passive and civilised to be able to defend themselves against militarised factions or repressive laws.

If mass radicalism is a usual concomitant of industrialisation, would one expect the newly emerging countries to produce such movements? Clearly one would, especially since the rise of communism on a peasant base will encourage attempts to form movements prior to urbanisation. As traditional ways become disrupted by modernisation the appeals of the mass movement will become more attractive. Mass movements have characteristically replaced religion as a source of spiritual attraction. They either grow out of revivalism, like the British labour movement, or out of anti-clericalism, like French and Italian Communism. It is noteworthy that the United States, the only major modernised society without a mass radical movement, also has one of the highest levels of Church attendance. The attempts to give a 'full life' within the movement clearly underline its role as a substitute for organised religion. The radical mass movement has a theology, a priesthood, collective worship and the offer of a tangible heaven. It would scarcely be surprising, then, if peasants removed from the traditional and religion sanctioned life of the village were not to be attracted to the mass movements of the cities in increasing numbers. It was this danger which alerted Bishop Ketteler in the 1870's and gave rise to organised Christian Democracy in Europe as an attempt to counter-organise against socialism.

There are certain modifications which must be made to any model proposing an inevitable rise in mass radicalism as urbanisation proceeds. In the first place the mass movement may not be radical in the nineteenth-century sense, but reactionary. Nazism is the clearest example of the possibility of mass action for reactionary purposes. In Argentina, with substantial urbanisation, the mass Peronist movement is at least ambivalent in its attitude to the traditional radical values. In India, where urbanisation is only beginning, there is a very real prospect of reactionary mass movements combining peasants and scarcely urbanised workers and clerks in defence of Hindu obscurantism. Similarly in Japan, now a fully industrialised country, the Sokka Gakei powerfully reasserts traditional values on a massive organisational basis. It is faced by the equally powerful socialist movements in a potential confrontation similar to that between Nazis, socialists and communists in Weimar Germany. Mass movements, then, are likely to grow and spread, but they will not necessarily have the same ideologies or general features as the mass radicalism discussed above. One would also expect to see the formation of 'pseudo' mass movements by dictators imitating totalitarian models. Thus in West Africa, where there is very little industrial development, organisations like the Convention Peoples Party have, nevertheless, grown, and may grow again if suitably encouraged. It is doubtful, however, whether they will grow as spontaneously from below as movements in more advanced systems have done in the past, and whether they will survive the downfall of the particular group which brought them into being.

Mass movements have grown, and will continue to grow, out of the shocks of industrialisation. What of the now long established mass parties based on these past eruptions? Here one is likely to witness decline, as movement characteristics become increasingly disfunctional. The terminology of mass radical parties in Western Europe has already become a source of embarrassment to most of the leaders. The repeated 'betrayals' of the past sixty years, which have marked adjustment to acceptance within the established framework, are still resented by the radicals but accepted by the conservatives within the movements. Just as the masses turned from religion to politics, so they are now turning from politics to mass entertainment and the comforts of home. The communal life of the factory and slum is replaced by the fragmented and home-centred life of the suburb. Mass radical movements wither. Like the Church of England, their main efforts are devoted to keeping alive. With the exception of Italy, which is still industrialising, the mass radical movements are facing decay all over Europe. They are, at the same time professionalising their propaganda and centralising their leadership. The part of the industrial working class in the movements diminishes, as that class itself declines and is absorbed into tertiary employment. One powerful reason for supposing that a mass radical movement will never arise in the United States is that this social trend has progressed furthest there. Sectional mass movements, like Civil Rights, will continue, but a movement successfully embracing the 'masses' as a whole becomes more remote by the hour.

6

Totalitarian parties

The twentieth century created a completely new form of political organisation, the totalitarian party. Reaching its most complete form in the German Nazi Party and the Soviet Communist Party, totalitarianism has been adopted in varying forms. Perhaps fortunately, these have rarely been able to achieve the degree of effectiveness of the two classic organisations. Nor have most of the single-party systems of the underdeveloped world adopted the full range of totalitarian practices. Some particularly brutal dictatorships, like that of Duvalier in Haiti, may have exceeded even Hitler's Germany or Stalin's Russia in the destruction of opponents, but not on the basis of a fully effective totalitarian party. Thus it is necessary to define the totalitarian party fairly strictly, to distinguish it from milder forms or from those which are only super-ficially similar. No two totalitarian parties have remained exactly alike for long, although most of the communist parties of Eastern Europe were consciously modelled on the Soviet Party in the 1940's and early 1950's. No two fascist parties have been alike, and some would deny the term totalitarian to the Italian Fascists or the Spanish Falange. Ideologically there is little in common between the two broad categories of fascist and communist movements. The resemblances are in the methods of operation, not in the terms used. Some of the appeals are basically to the same instinct and various totalitarian leaders seem to have had similar anxieties and obsessions. But to say that communism and fascism are both totalitarian forms is not to say that they are the same thing or will have the same consequences in the long run.

The totalitarian parties are, by definition, successful government parties. It is impossible to apply the full force of totalitarianism within the party unless armed force can be employed. There are, of course, many communist and fascist parties which do not reach power but they either remain in the first historic phase of the party's development or accommodate to their democratic environment as the Italian Communists are clearly doing and approximate to mass radical parties. The first phase is that of the struggling movement, attracting a high proportion of unstable people who move into and out of it, and dependent on a few dominant personalities to keep things going. The characteristic feature of those totalitarian movements which succeeded is that their rise was meteoric and their origins obscure and uninspiring. The Chinese Communist Party had fifty members in 1920 and has eighteen million today. The Nazi Party rose from seven to seven million members in twenty years. The Soviet Communist Party dates its first congress from 1898, when seven delegates attended, some of them undoubtedly police spies. It had already achieved a membership of one million just over twenty years later. Thus it is not too absurd for small and uninspiring groups like the Communist Party of Great Britain or the much more electorally successful National Democratic Party in Germany to be seen as the potential basis for a successful totalitarianism.

Characteristic of the early phase is the factionalism and instability of the movement. The complex jungle of relationships in the Russian Marxist movement is matched, on a much lower intellectual level, by the vicious factionalism of the fascist groups in Weimar Germany. The

same instability is found throughout the communist movement in its first twenty years. In later years the rise of
paid officials gave even the smallest communist parties
a permanent backbone and lessened the appearance of
factionalism. The membership remained extremely unstable, mostly young and attracted from individuals and
social groups who felt alienated from society for various
reasons. This attraction of social deviants has been most
apparent in the fascist movements. When such people
get into power, as they did in Hitler's Germany, they make
totalitarianism an instrument for the most perverse forms
of repression witnessed in the modern era. There is also
a strong tendency to paranoia or delusions of grandeur
among the few charismatic leaders who have driven these
small parties along, although this is not completely lack-
ing in many other political leaders. During this first phase
the putative totalitarian movement develops its basic
characteristic of a secular religion, with solidarity based
on fears of real or imagined persecution and devotion to a
leader as an earthly saviour. Without Lenin, Hitler or
Mussolini it is hard to imagine their fractious and unstable
followings having the drive to get into power. Already,
then, in the early phases, totalitarian attitudes are bred
from belief in the truth of the ideology, fear of persecution, reactions against indiscipline, hatred of the outsider,
and obedience to a dominant leader.

Where the movement is not submerged under a competitive party system, but succeeds in the revolution which
its messianic aims makes necessary, it moves into its
second and most influential phase. It carries out the role
of government party with the aura of the revolution
attaching to itself, and with all political positions under
its patronage. The party starts to grow rapidly as it becomes the sole agency through which promotion can be
gained. Élites are remoulded as those raised in the pre-
revolutionary environment are weeded out. This may
mean a complete change in the sources of political recruit-

81

ment. In the Soviet Union in the 1920's those of 'bourgeois social origin' were excluded from higher education and government positions, while the Communist Party began the intensive training in party schools which created leaders like Khruschev. The convention was thus established over ten years from 1917 that the party was the road to success, not only in formal politics but in management, the professions and the armed forces. The new class of bureaucrats, against whom Trotsky railed from 1923 onwards, came to dominate the party. They were essentially of working class and peasant origin, educated out of their class by virtue of party membership and encouragement. This retraining of a whole new élite was not carried so far in Nazi Germany, was even less apparent in Fascist Italy, and not apparent in Spain or Portugal at all. The degree of totalitarianism in a system can be measured, among other things, by the extent to which the victorious party does become the sole avenue to promotion.

The third phase of the totalitarian party is that where the party itself has become firmly established and starts to throw off its now superfluous pioneers. Hitler began this process almost immediately with the execution of Rohm and other Stormtroop leaders in 1934. The Stormtroopers, whose militarised violence had been essential to Nazi success, were demoted and disarmed, being replaced by Hitler's personal bodyguard, the S.S., and by the official State police, the Gestapo. In communist states the process was slower but essentially similar. Stalin began to ease his opponents out of party positions in 1925, to expel them by 1927 and to execute them by 1936. By 1939 he had achieved the extermination of the great bulk of 'Old Bolsheviks', those who had been in the party before 1917. The communists had no armed guards comparable to the Stormtroopers. But the Red Army, which had been created by Trotsky and the Party in 1919, had its general staff wiped out in 1937. As in Germany the official state police, the N.K.V.D., was given authority over the party. By 1939 the Soviet Communist Party and the German Nazi Party were both reduced to puppets in the hands of their leaders, who used the state machine quite brutally to retain their power. The parties still had the role of maintaining mass enthusiasm but were submerged in the state machine and by large youth, labour and women's front organisations. Stalin virtually suspended the decision-making role of the party, holding only three party congresses in the last twenty years of his life and almost abandoning central committee meetings. The same processes were followed in Eastern Europe between 1949 and 1952.

There is no way of telling what would have happened to the nazi and fascist parties had they not been destroyed in the war. In Spain, thirty years after the civil war, the Falange is a very subordinate body to the organs of church and state and there is some suggestion that Italian fascism was moving in the same direction. The fascist victories in Latin and East European countries were not so clearly party victories as were Hitler's and Lenin's and the traditional élites were left largely undisturbed. In Nazi Germany the sheer degeneracy and manifest insanity of many Nazi leaders suggest the difficulty of the movement being anything other than self-destructive. In the Soviet Union and Eastern Europe however, communism inherited a more humane tradition, whatever its actual practices. After Stalin's death the communist parties have entered a new phase. They have reasserted their dynamism, while at the same time permitting the modification of the totalitarian states they have set up. It cannot be said that the parties have done this whole-heartedly. They seem to be more conservative than many youthful or highly educated reformers who have been pressing for change. Such change must still come through the party and it could not have done so had the typically atrophied party of Stalin's period, subjugated to the secret police, not been allowed to re-invigorate itself.

This fourth phase of revival of the party and relaxation of state controls is most closely associated with the name of Khruschev. He attempted to bring back life to the decadent party and to turn it into a driving force once more, instead of an agency for promotion and propaganda only. In quite a different way the Red Guards and Maoists in China are attempting to purge the bureaucrats and recreate the party as a secular religion once again. If this succeeds, which is currently doubtful, then Chinese totalitarianism will move in a fundamentally different direction from European. For there are signs that after the Khruschev phase the Soviet-bloc parties are now entering a new era. The Yugoslavs have led the way with their declarations that in due course the party will wither away and be replaced by direct popular initiative. This is much closer to syndicalism than to classic Leninism and is disturbing to the Soviet leaders. In Yugoslavia, Poland and Hungary the party has deliberately reduced its political monopoly by allowing conflicting candidatures at elections, although these are vetted by the party. This has led to genuine electoral competition though without the formation of competing parties. On the example of Turkey and Mexico, it is quite possible for a single-party system to relax to the extent where multi-partyism grows naturally out of it. This is not yet the intention of official East European communists but it is being discussed by younger radicals throughout the area. The latest phase of totalitarianism is one in which the Yugoslav and Polish parties are no longer as rigidly disciplined, as exclusive and ideologically pure as the classic model would suppose. Romania, too, seems to be moving in the same direction.

The totalitarian model

The above discussion has assumed, as most writers do, that totalitarianism is confined to the fascist and communist parties, and especially their European versions. Totalitarianism, while it may have inspired some leaders in the underdeveloped countries, is essentially a product of inter-war Europe, based on the social disruption which the war brought. It was not the parties themselves that caused the disruption. Russia, Germany and Italy were already in social chaos when the parties succeeded. Thus while there may be putative totalitarian parties anywhere in the world, they are never likely to leave the first stage unless social conditions for their success are present. These conditions include severe wartime destruction, economic collapse, lack of faith in existing élites, and alienation of large sections of the population from existing political practices. Some writers go further and suggest that national psychology or child-rearing patterns may make a country more susceptible to totalitarianism. It is very hard to explain why an advanced and civilised nation like Germany succumbed so readily to such unattractive creatures as the Nazi leaders. But the present writer is sceptical about attempts to answer this problem mainly in the field of social psychology. Leaders of totalitarian movements are rarely 'normal', and once in power can impose their attitudes on any nation unfortunate enough to permit it.

Given that communism and fascism appear antithetical there are some difficulties in treating the movements under a common heading. Writers like Talmon, in *The Origins of Totalitarian Democracy*, have been able to find common intellectual origins in social contract theory while others have stressed the common ancestry of Hegel and idealism. This is undoubtedly a fruitful approach because so much of what totalitarian parties have done has been dictated by their view of the true nature of man. Political philosophers cannot, of course, explain why totalitarianism has succeeded in one country rather than another, nor why it found certain methods necessary to achieve its ends. It remains an important truth, however, that totalitarians believe that man has a true nature which must be freed from the artificial shackles imposed by existing social

85

arrangements. Many anarchists and socialists believe the same without becoming totalitarians. There remains a temptation, once having accepted the role of releasing man's true nature, to accomplish this desirable, if illusory, goal by force. Thus a basic feature of the totalitarian party is that it is based on secular religious beliefs and drives which persuade its members of their collective messianic role, whether to save mankind or simply the race. Once persuaded of this, the movement's founders attract support without forcing unanimity, because that unanimity will be as freely given as it is to the more rigorous religious sects. The totalitarian party is not simply based on an ideology, because the same could be said in varying degrees for most parties. It is based on a complete commitment to beliefs which are held to be totally consistent and totally true and urgently requiring translation into reality. Thus totalitarian parties always devote much energy to re-educating their members in the ideology and to insulating them from distracting influences.

Along with ideological commitment, or the creation of 'professional revolutionaries' to use Lenin's term, goes rigid discipline. This is ideally achieved by voluntary commitment to the collective. Where this breaks down the member is expelled or, if the party is in power, is executed. The parties are militarised, basing most of their collective action on marching, carrying banners or holding rallies. They are often in uniform and their youth groups almost invariably are. Despite the quite different attitudes to party democracy possessed by fascists and communists, in practice both kinds of party are based on rigorous obedience to the leadership and normally on hero worship as well as party worship. Life outside the movement becomes unthinkable and social life, marriage, education and childrearing takes place within a party-organised framework. Expelled members are ostracised and smeared if not physically attacked. There is nothing in this which has not been found before in religious denominations and, in very modified form, in other mass parties on the central European model. Submission to the collective will is a common feature of human organisation. Totalitarianism simply carries this to the extreme of not permitting any questioning or deviation which interferes with the immediate, earthly attainment of essentially metaphysical objectives like total human harmony.

Hierarchy, discipline and total commitment are the three essentials of any totalitarian movement. In the phase before achieving power these characteristics are in danger of erosion by outside influences. Party members leave as there is no incentive to stay in and no force to prevent their resignation. As many totalitarian movements have actually been persecuted they are able to hold their dedicated members together in opposition to the outside threat. Where that threat is weak it must be exaggerated by the party. In the rare cases where communist movements have become established as permanent features of a democratic system, they can only retain their exclusiveness by playing on the sense of social alienation of their followers. If this starts to decline then the party must come to terms with its new role. It is no longer totalitarian but just a more rigidly disciplined and dogmatic socialist party.

When the party is in power its character changes. It can draw on the talent of the entire nation, not simply on the discontented and rebellious. Because it is engaged in social engineering on a scale not previously attempted, it permeates institutions which most other parties leave alone. A central feature of totalitarianism is its creation of military forces which are distinct from the formal army and police, and are subject to the party and its leaders. The Nazi Party had great difficulty in gaining acceptance for this from the Army but by the end of the war S.S. units were engaged on the Eastern Front. On the

Soviet side the problem was not so acute. The Red Army was created by the Party and has always been the subject of permeation by political commissars. Military officers are normally communists, in contrast to the reluctance of some German officers to join the Nazi Party. Thus, while there are party political intrusions on the armed forces in many countries, in totalitarian states they are an essential feature of party control. It is also essential that the mass media be controlled by the party. All editorships in communist states come under party nomination while most important newspapers are owned either by the state or by the party. Again this was not achieved as fully in Germany but there was little scope for the press and none for the radio to remain free from Nazi influence.

In addition to controlling the armed forces and the mass media, the governing totalitarian party normally nominates for offices throughout a wider range than in other systems. This makes it peculiarly vulnerable to careerists and constant purging must be maintained to ensure that the party does not degenerate completely. Efforts are made to see that the party does not become submerged in the state machine but retains its identity. To the extent that the party fails to maintain its superiority over the state it becomes an agency of government and increasingly superfluous. This was happening in Mussolini's Italy and has happened much more quickly in one-party African states which were never truly totalitarian despite some attempts to copy the model.

The party sets itself above the state and sets its ideology above all other secular and religious alternatives. In fact religion often continues to secure loyalty and may have to be compromised with as Hitler did with the Lutheran and Catholic Churches and Stalin with Orthodoxy during the war. The aim of the party is normally to supplant such beliefs among the young. It was the failure or refusal of fascist parties to do this in Catholic countries which is one reason for denying them the title of totalitarian. In order to educate the young the party normally monopolises the field of youth organisation. Thus while it may not form a very large proportion of the total population, it will normally control nearly all the organised youth and will ban alternative groups. The same is true of labour unions and women's organisations, although the latter are not always taken so seriously. The key to totalitarianism is that all alternative forms of and bases for organisation are dominated by the party which excludes others from the area. All politically sensitive positions are held by party members and all armed force is under party supervision or control. This makes it possible for a system to be totally controlled by a very small proportion of the people. While Mussolini's Italy, like Touré's Guinea, aimed to enroll the whole population within the party, the nazis and communists have been more élitist. The average proportion of Communist Party members in communist states is now just over 5% of total population, ranging from 2.5% in China to 12% in Czechoslovakia. Within this proportion a very high percentage come from management, the armed forces and police and the full-time party bureaucrats.

As totalitarian parties settle down to the tasks of government they tend to become more conservative and to have problems of sustaining the enthusiasm and religious devotion which once kept them together. Loyalty to the party becomes, like loyalty to a business corporation, a matter of promotion and privileged employment. The party itself becomes a major source of employment. Virtually all its decision makers above local level are party or party-nominated employees. The party officials are totally enmeshed within the state machine, despite consistent attempts to prevent them from being submerged altogether. Once the basic restructuring of society is completed and the permanent atmosphere of crisis abates, the totalitarian party becomes a naturally cautious and self-protecting organisation. It loses the resilience and drive it once had and fails to attract the youth for idealistic reasons. These problems are central to the efforts of the Soviet Communist Party to re-organise itself in the past ten years. It tries to reinforce its identity as a leading force by constantly recruiting new members from the technologists. In fact it has become completely transformed in fifty years from a party of the revolutionary and alienated, urged on by messianic beliefs, into the agency for promotion in a highly technical and advanced industrial system.

The future of totalitarianism

Most writing about totalitarianism until very recently has tended to depict it as an almost unavoidable feature of mass society under strain, with its alienated men searching for leadership and meaning. The totalitarian party was seen as almost unique in that it did not soften with age as other mass parties have done, that it gave no opening for debate or disagreement within its ranks, that it was incapable of defeat except by violent means. Between 1945 and 1955, with the practice of Stalin and the memory of Hitler still fresh, this fear of totalitarianism and belief in its invincibility seemed reasonable. It is now clear that totalitarian parties also accommodate themselves to the system within which they operate and are also subject to change and decay in the same way as other parties, if more slowly and with greater heart searching. This is not to argue that communist and fascist parties are essentially like other mass parties, which would be absurd. Rather it is to question whether the constant mobilisation and activism which characterises such parties is anything more than a long drawn out response to crises. As under Stalin these crises may be created by the party leaders themselves and are an important factor in maintaining the totalitarian features of the party. Constant crises and the

frenetic style of politics they involve tend to become unattractive to even the most devoted party and state
officials. Both Hitler and Stalin frequently brought their
systems to disaster and were constantly threatened by dis-
sension which they had to crush at the expense of the
vitality of their own movements. The same tendency of
totalitarians to destroy their own colleagues is apparent
from China where respected party ideologues like Liu Shao
Chi are being denigrated by the very movement they
created.

This self-destructive nature of totalitarian parties gives
them only two alternatives. Either they must crush themselves, as the nazis and fascists did, by engaging in a war
beyond their capacity, or they must gradually dismantle
the crisis style of politics, as the communists are beginning to do in the Soviet Union and Eastern Europe. This
was quite naturally not so clear in the 1930's and 1940's
when there was a continuous world crisis on which
totalitarianism was able to feed. It is remarkable that not
only in Europe, but also in the underdeveloped world,
the past twenty years have not seen anything comparable. Communist successes in China and Vietnam, as in
Cuba, have been the result of military operations. Few
mass communist parties, and even fewer fascist parties,
have been able to establish themselves. Only in France,
Italy and Finland have European Communist Parties continued to dominate the labour movement. Even there
they have accommodated themselves to democratic politics and modified their crisis mentality and totalitarian
practices to some extent. In the rest of the world the
Indian Communists are not totalitarian in any sense
of the word, the Indonesian Communists were crushed
easily by the Army in 1966, and only in one or two Latin-
American countries have communist or syndicalist movements been able to play an important role. This is not
to deny that the conscious efforts of American aid programmes and other forms of Western intervention may

not have lessened the appeal of totalitarian parties. It is to suggest that the classic communist and nazi form of organisation now seems peculiar to inter-war Europe and much less likely to spread than seemed probable only ten years ago. Very few of the mass single parties of Africa come anywhere near the degree of cohesion and discipline which characterised the European movements. The only one which did, the Convention Peoples Party of Ghana, now lies as effectively in ruins before the Army as does the Communist Party in Indonesia.

It is early yet to prophesy that totalitarianism will have no further appeal in developing countries. The disruptions caused by war or by rapid industrialisation may yet re-create the conditions of the 1930's. However, students of totalitarianism like Friedrich or Arendt have stressed that it is found in technologically advancing states and relies on the mass media and the availability of alienated urban masses for its success. Thus the essentially peasant economies of most of the world seem unfruitful bases for such a highly organised secular religion, especially as the rural masses are still dominated by spiritual religions for which they need no substitute as yet. Where urbanisation has proceeded, as in Japan, there are signs of a conservative reaction, and this has also been noted among rural masses migrating to urban centres in the United States. Urbanisation in Latin America may also stimulate semi-totalitarian movements of a Peronist or Aprista nature. In India the Jan Sangh and the Dravida Munnetra Kazhagham are growing in strength on the basis of some totalitarian methods and attempts at discipline. Nothing comparable to Hitlerism or Stalinism has arisen, in the sense of militarily disciplined movements prepared to shift vast sectors of the population and to destroy them if necessary in the name of the party's ideals. Perhaps only a technically advanced state with a relatively civilised and docile people would be likely to submit to such monstrous forms of organisation. Communist China seemed to be moving in that direction, but has now severely disrupted the Communist Party itself and, as in so many other countries, fallen back on the army to change existing arrangements and to clean out the bureaucrats.

7

Parties in the underdeveloped world

There are now over one hundred party systems in the world and most of these are in the underdeveloped countries. This has greatly increased the possible combinations of parties, their organisational variety and programmatic differences. However, most parties have been formed by Western-educated leaders and have borrowed freely from Western examples. Indeed there are very few instances of truly indigenous political parties and movements. Even specifically traditionalist ethnic parties like the Jan Sangh or Akali Dal in India, the Panmalayan Islamic Party in Malaya or the Kabaka Yekka in Uganda have tended to copy some Western practices. Those states least affected by colonialism, like Saudi Arabia, Thailand, Yemen or Nepal, have either not produced parties at all or have done so simply by attaching party labels to ruling families and their retainers. There is no organisational form of party peculiar to the 'third world' which has not already appeared in the developed countries at some stage except perhaps the guerilla party. What is distinct is the extent to which traditional élites, linguistic groups, families and tribes have formed the basis of parties. Class based politics on the Western model has been rare. In looking at politics in underdeveloped countries we must not lose sight of the fact that superficially Western terms and practices may disguise quite different realities. The political party is a Western invention. Its transference to traditional societies has nowhere been accomplished without basic changes from the original model. This is true even for such rigid models as the Leninist. In recent years the Communist Party of China has been behaving in a manner totally inconsistent with classic Soviet practice. The Indian and Indonesian Communists have never truly conformed with the European pattern. If this is true for such a standardised organisation as the Communist Party, it is even more true of the various socialist and liberal parties which have been set up in the past twenty-five years.

The most common types found in the 'third world' have been loosely organised combinations of local committees, with loyalty to families, individuals or tribal and linguistic groups as the main cement. Coherent ideologies have been relatively unimportant, despite the commitment to 'socialism' of the great majority of third world parties. The potentially totalitarian party has had only moderate success as has the mass party typical of both social-democracy and European conservatism. These two kinds of highly integrated party seem to need an urban base which is largely absent in Africa and Asia. Moreover their functioning depends to some extent on loyalty being given to the party in exchange for the right to some mass participation in decision making. Where loyalty to traditional symbols and leaders remains important it is difficult to transfer this to the party without added inducements like patronage. Moreover, mass participation in a democratic process presupposes the literacy and information to make such activity fruitful and even possible, and the financial resources to subscribe to party funds in exchange for these rights. Even where mass parties appear to exist, as in India or Indonesia, it is often found that they are not based on the vast subscribing membership which they claim. The supporters are adherents in the same sense as registered Democrats or Republicans in the United States. There is an inner core paying higher dues and taking

95

part in decision making, while the vast outer member-ship is enrolled in youth wings or front organisations which collectively subscribe to or work for the party.

There are a substantial number of the smaller nations which either do not have parties at all, or have had them abolished by military coup. The withering away of parties in tropical Africa has been most apparent. This process is caused either by the educated minority who dominate the party becoming absorbed in the government bureau-cracy of a one-party state, or by the army replacing the party as the disciplined group at the centre of decision making. Thus in tropical Africa, parts of the Middle East, and the least Westernised countries of South East Asia, there are now no party systems worthy of the name. Nor is there any immediate sign of their revival. Aid pro-grammes directed at building up armies and bureaucracies have worked against the development of parties. As these aid programmes are often specifically designed to counter or even suppress socialist or populist parties, this has further inhibited spontaneous growth even in democracies where this is possible. The party now often appears as a transitional phase, making it easier to replace the tradi-tional aristocratic élites by the newly educated civil ser-vants and generals. Once this process has been completed the party no longer has a function and disappears or is abolished. Where there are no longer elections and office is gained by violence or nepotism, it is hard to see what function a non-revolutionary party could fufil in small countries with a very limited politically involved élite. Should such countries industrialise and expand their educa-tion, then parties will probably arise once more to give a voice to new segments clamouring for access to decision making.

A more successful type of party is commonly found in rather larger states with some urbanisation and a wide, educated élite. This is the single mass party used by the government as a transmission belt for communicating with the people, as a recruitment area for the large number of posts to be filled, as a propaganda agency for defending the government, and as a prop to other centres of power like the army and the police. Such parties are found in their classical form in Egypt and Burma. In both cases the 'socialist' parties were formed by the army and replaced previously existing civilian parties like the Wafd or the Anti-Fascist Peoples Freedom League. This type of party is also found in Latin America and may be compared to the Falange Party of Spain. In all cases it is not the party which effectively wields power, in contrast to the totalitarian situation. The party is handmaiden of the army or the Church, carrying out functions which they cannot or will not undertake. The party may eventually become an alternative source of power, critical of the régime as some Falangists have become in Spain. At present, the effective controllers of the country are contemptuous of civilian party politics and use the mass party as a channel for energies which might otherwise go, in frustration, into other kinds of party.

The other type of single party is that where power and patronage do appear to stem primarily from the party itself. This was true of the mass-mobilising parties of Ghana and Guinea, of the Ba'ath Socialist Party in the Arab world, of the Chinese Communist Party or the Tanzanian African National Union. Army and police forces stand behind these parties and may, as the Ghanaian and possibly Chinese cases show, resent them and even overthrow them or some of their leaders. This type of party may have totalitarian aspirations. It chooses the policy makers, elevates the national leaders, penetrates the organs of repression, controls the mass media and dispenses patronage in general. This latter function may lead to such wholesale corruption that the dedication and puritanism of this type of party becomes completely eroded. Until this does happen, or until army resentment becomes too strong to be contained, the mass party of this sort seems able to hold its own. It becomes a focus for national integration, bringing in classes and tribes who had previously been excluded from politics. It is this integrating possibility which has made it so attractive to some of the more sophisticated African countries. However, mass parties are rarely free from some degree of preference for certain segments of society however self-consciously they strive after equality of opportunity. In particular they tend to represent the interests of the newly educated as against those of both the traditional leaders and the uneducated masses.

These mass parties function in one-party situations, the most common form of arrangement in the third world. However, it would be foolish to overlook the fact that as many people live under competitive democracy in the underdeveloped countries as do in the advanced nations. Some six hundred million people, mainly in India, Brazil and South-East Asia, live under effectively functioning multi-party systems, a total equivalent to those in the temperate industrial countries of Europe, North America, Australasia and Japan. It is in these competitive democracies that one would expect to find parties closest to the Western models. However, this is only superficially true. The parties of the Philippines or South Korea bear terminological resemblances to those of the United States on which they are based. The British labour movement has encouraged parties in Malaysia and India, the Caribbean and East and Central Africa and they have dutifully adopted the appropriate terminology. Even such an apparently indigenous movement as the Indian National Congress was founded partly by English liberals. One of its early presidents, Dadabhai Naoroji sat in the British House of Commons, while all its national presidents until the recent election of Kamaraj have spoken English fluently.

These obvious links with the former colonists may lead to false conclusions about the way in which parties operate. If there is still any resemblance between the Philippine and American parties it is largely that they are ideologically indistinct and based on patronage as an inducement to activism. However, it is more fruitful to compare the Philippine parties with the American city machines at the turn of the century than with the great national parties of today. The Indian National Congress can scarcely be understood in British terms at all today, nor, indeed, could it have been at any time since its transformation into a mass organisation in 1921. It is neither a centre, nor a socialist, nor a conservative party. It is neither a traditional nor a modernising party. It is not a party of integration, though one which integrates by pertion with no ideals. It comes closest to being a national party of integration though one which integrates by persuasion and compromise in a multi-party situation rather than by the more restrictive and thus easier methods of the African single party. It is extremely hard to see how any national party in India could fail to be based on this approach. The various communist and socialist parties are equally riven by linguistic and caste disagreements. Only the specifically ethnic parties like the Dravida Munnetra Kazhagham, the Jan Sangh, or the Akali Dal, seem to be able to mobilise their supporters effectively. Congress could do so as a national movement against the British, but cannot as the dominant party of a multi-national state.

Thus at all levels Western models are simply shells into which the traditional social and political forces of the third world have been poured. This has forced even the most enthusiastic modernisers, the university educated socialists and communists, to compromise with the very forces which they are pledged to destroy. Nevertheless, the rule of the traditional aristocracies has been seriously disturbed and they too must adopt the form of party if their interests are not to be completely submerged. Thus the sultans of Malaya are forced into common cause with the Chinese and Indian merchants of the Alliance, the northern emirs of Nigeria have their own party and the Moslem ulemas form or support parties from Sudan to

Indonesia. As in the formative period of political institutions in the advanced states, so in the underdeveloped countries, parties are both shaped by their societies and shape them by recruiting new leaders and opening up new avenues of power for the previously excluded.

Traditionalism

The mass party is a modern institution based on the assumption that men are politically rational and can collectively shape the destinies of a state. Even in the most urbanised and literate nations constant compromise with irrationality and prejudice is forced on the party by its need to retain mass support or even the support of its supposedly enlightened members. Thus the Republican Party in the United States found itself swept into support for Senator Goldwater by prejudiced and irrational forces which even the Senator must have found embarrassing. Both British parties were shifted from lofty assumptions of racial tolerance by the electors of the West Midlands. In every European and North American country it is increasingly obvious that factors such as religion, language, racial prejudice cut across the economic rationality of electors and party members. Voting, thinking and acting along class lines might itself, of course, be regarded by some conservatives as irrational, educated as they are to believe that the rational man perceives the superiority of the élite. Thus, however purist an ideology a party may espouse, it finds it difficult to ignore forces among the people which it might deplore. Parties may try to stand against these tendencies but are often influenced against the will of their enlightened leaders and active members.

It is not surprising, then, that the parties of the underdeveloped world while being largely modernising in their aspirations, have often succumbed to traditionalist and conservative influences. This has been studied most fully in India, where political leaders are normally highly educated but where three-quarters of the population are rural illiterates. While there is no reason to suppose that Indians are less capable of making rational electoral choices than anyone else, there is a serious problem for the Indian politician in mobilising his followers behind modernising slogans which they instinctively reject. Despite poverty and famine, it has been the conservative and reactionary parties which have made most recent progress, rather than the socialists and communists. Communism only succeeds in the most educationally advanced areas like Kerala and West Bengal. Throughout India the modernising parties of the Left have been only too willing to enter alliances with the obscurantists and linguistic patriots which, in Western terms, make little sense. This interaction between tradition and modernity has always typified the mass political movements of India as of other under-developed nations.

Even in its origins as a largely upper-middle class Western educated discussion society, the Indian National Congress soon found it necessary to accept traditionalist support if it wanted to widen its base. Thus the Ganapati movement in Maharashtra and the associated Shivaji revival movement in the 1890's were the vehicles by which the radicals in Congress led by Tilak became prominent. The equally radical Chandra Bhose in the 1930's owed some of his support to Kali worshippers in Bengal. There is still a small political sect in Calcutta, the Forward Bloc, some of whose members believe that Bhose did not die in 1944 but will return in a messianic role when the time is ripe. Throughout the history of Congress there has been this constant interrelationship between traditionalism and radi-calism. Today, when the traditionalists have formed parties of their own and the socialists and communists are also severed from Congress, these apparently contradictory alliances are even more open in the form of coalitions in State politics. Even within Congress itself, a major force in the defeat of Krishna Menon in Bombay in 1967 was the Shivaji Army, owing its origins to Tilak's movement to revive the cult of the Marathi national hero.

This intrusion of traditionalism is apparent throughout Asia. In Ceylon, where three-quarters of Members of Parliament are university educated, one party leader, a former Marxist, opened his 1965 campaign at the shrine of Skandar, while the Prime Minister, Mrs. Bandaranaike, began hers at the ancient Buddhist site of Anuradhapura. Nor is this surprising when one remembers the prayers before parliament, the blessing of candidates, the hymns at party conferences, which typify even such a secular party system as that of Britain. The important difference is that, whereas in most advanced countries the appeal to religion, nationalism or tradition is currently secondary to economic appeals, in the underdeveloped world, despite its much greater poverty, the opposite is true. There is more congruence between the aims, education and aspirations of party leaders and followers in developed nations than in the underdeveloped. Grave difficulties of communication force the educated élite to use the appeals of obscurantism however unpalatable they may find them.

Patronage

The mass party has been a major force in broadening political recruitment. Even the British Conservative Party, with its incredibly narrow social range at the top, has brought groups into local and sometimes national politics who would have been excluded before the extension of the franchise and the rise of mass parties. The radical parties fulfil this function more obviously. In the underdeveloped nations this role remains extremely important. The problem of political recruitment is a dual one. In the first place, in colonial countries, there is the need to build up a new élite altogether, not just in the new representative institutions, but also in the bureaucracy, the army and in education and often business as well. Not surprisingly, many of these posts are subject to party patronage even where, as in former British colonies, an attempt to import a non-partisan approach to recuitment has been made. The other aspect of recruitment is that the great bulk of positions not held by expatriates are often held by traditional aristocrats, subsidised or maintained by the colonial power. The first task of the newly-independent government is to abolish or reduce in importance these traditional rulers and replace them by partisan nominees. Thus the Indian princes were bought out and replaced by Congress nominated State governors. In the case of Mysore he was, in fact, the former Maharajah. In the Malay states the sultans remain but are less important than the Alliance state politicians. In Ghana the Convention Peoples Party had to fight against the Ashanti chiefs, in Uganda the Peoples Party had to combat the Kabaka of Buganda, and other chiefs. The conflict will resolve itself in four possible ways, all involving party. Either the national party will genuinely replace the aristocrats with totally new nominees, or it will incorporate the aristocracy into its ranks and leave them fairly intact, or the aristocracy will form parties of their own to protect their interests or they will join such parties, as Indian princes are joining Swatantra and Jan Sangh.

The totalitarian or mass-mobilising party is the most likely to conflict with the aristocracy, the loosely integrated party of notables the most likely to accommodate them. This has, of course, been equally true in Europe at an earlier stage. In general, the very fact that parties arise as important agents of political recruitment is likely to mean some dilution of the old élites, if not their total destruction. Very often, of course, the newly educated Westernised reformers are the sons of the old élite, while in other cases they come from professional and mercantile classes already given some access to power by the colonialists. In very few countries, developed or otherwise, could it be argued that parties have acted effectively as agents for the mass of the population to send its sons into positions of power. Perhaps only in the Soviet Union and one or two East European countries, experiencing many years of war and revolution, has the new élite been drawn from substantially different social origins than the old. Political parties tend to be controlled by the professional classes in all countries. In the U.S.S.R. the new class of engineers dominates the party. In most underdeveloped nations it is still the lawyers, teachers, public servants and, in some cases, the military officers who dominate, much as they did in nineteenth-century Europe.

The fact that parties are such major instruments for recruitment, albeit from already well-established classes, makes it almost inevitable that they should be subject to nepotism, to favouritism and to exclusiveness. This is particularly clear in nations which have more than one major language, race or religious group. In India the entire party system is riddled with caste and family preference, which makes factional, rather than party conflict, the major force at local level. While it is more difficult to sub-stantiate findings in one party states, it is apparent that some of the 'parties of national integration' also give pre-ference to some sections of the nation over others. The dissolution of Nigeria became imminent because of the open favouritism in recruitment which was sustained by the party system. It is not surprising therefore that so many parties in multi-party situations are clearly based on minorities. The language agitations in South India and Ceylon give the clearest examples of the effect of re-cruitment grievances on the party system. In both countries the Tamil-speaking populations felt that their strong posi-tions in the public services were being threatened by the enforcement of an official language other than English or their own. The Dravida Munnetra Kazhagham in Mad-ras state rapidly extended its support on a purely Tamil nationalist base. Combining modern and traditional drives, the D.M.K. originated from anti-Brahmin feelings among

Tamil Hindus but soon became the vehicle both for the existing and potential state employees and the Tamil language film industry. The Federal Party in Ceylon similarly defended the Tamil language as a method of defending recruitment into government posts.

Parties in underdeveloped countries are centrally interested in providing patronage or in protecting the patronage already extended to the cultural groups on which they are based. Purely revolutionary parties, aiming at the total restructuring of society, are much rarer than is often supposed, partly because such movements are repressed partly because, when not repressed, they begin to accommodate to the system and to the demands for patronage of their own supporters and members. Thus class-based mass movements are uncommon particularly those predominantly working-class parties which arose in conditions of massive industrialisation and urbanisation. Even where parties claim to be socialist, communist or populist, they are normally dominated by leaders from the professional or commercial classes, as indeed are such overtly working class organisations as the trade unions. In few underdeveloped countries have mass parties arisen which project substantial numbers of manual workers or poor peasants into political power, nor would one expect this until a much greater degree of urbanisation has taken place. The parties of the 'third world' are socialist to the extent that they want national socialism, the control of resources by nationals of the country, by the educated minority who felt themselves excluded from power by the colonial rulers. This minority, particularly that large part of it in Africa which comes from teachers and minor civil servants, may be of fairly humble origins. But it is education rather than the party alone which normally elevates them to positions of importance. The totalitarian party, which creates and educates completely new élites is very rare and, like the Convention Peoples Party in Ghana, very mild by European standards.

8

Conclusions

Parties are relatively fluid and often impermanent institutions. They aim at objectives which are believed to be attainable within the lifetime of their supporters. They are much more liable to change and adaptation than religious denominations, even where movements have tried to become secular religions based on revealed truths. Of all political institutions, parliaments included, the party is closest to the people, most susceptible to popular demands, most vulnerable to shifts in popular favour. This is obviously most true of competitive parties. The single party, with its cries of 'Nkrumah will live for ever!' or 'Forward under the everlasting banner of Communism' is less immediately responsive to popular demands. It may in its totalitarian form, even override and crush large sectors of the population which oppose it, destroying many of its own members in the process. Nevertheless the party remains a transmission belt. Even when it has become a vested interest with patronage and control as its main inspiration, it cannot remain uninfluenced by changes of mood in society. This is very clear from the experience of communism particularly in Eastern Europe and, more hesitantly, in the Soviet Union as well. When Khruschev 'restored the Leninist norms of party life' he was opening the only avenue to mass influence which exists in the Soviet Union, an avenue firmly closed by Stalin in the purges of the

1930's. The Soviet party incorporates almost the entire educated and influential élite of society and cannot superimpose its world view intact and for ever on its own members, the leaders of society.

The forces in a society are not necessarily liberal or beneficial. Party government is responsive to all forms of pressure. The forces may be reactionary, obscurantist or vicious. The support of masses of the German people in the early 1930's, of the majority of white South Africans today, of millions of Alabamans, Argentinians or Indonesians, of thousands of West Midland voters, has been given to voluntary movements whose aims are deplored by all liberal democrats. The claim cannot be made then that parties are an instrument of enlightenment, but simply that they are necessary in the struggle of broad masses of the people to influence political affairs in whatever direction they may choose. The free exercise of the franchise without parties is unthinkable in all competitive democracies in whatever kind of society. The free discussion of political affairs requires at the very least a loose single party, but preferably competing parties, if it is to be protected from repression. The recruitment of previously excluded segments of the population into politics is impossible without a party to achieve this objective either through patronage or through pressure against nepotism and privilege.

The party gives force to social philosophies and may attempt to turn them into reality. Because of the constant need to accommodate to social reality ideals may never be achieved or may lead to totalitarian distortions. These destroy their own objective by giving the masses what they 'need', but may not want. Nevertheless, parties with mildly ideological aspirations, however modified, have been a major force in shaping their societies and probably the only means which allows the general population some say in this shaping. Even the indistinct parties have been vehicles for social philosophies, as the Democrats were

107

under Roosevelt, or the Republicans under Goldwater. The distinctive and ideological parties not only served the interests of their supporters. They also transformed into reality some of the aspirations of those who adhered to parties for idealistic reasons. Those adherents may have been bitterly disappointed. They could scarcely deny that Russia without the Communist Party, Britain, Scandinavia and Australasia without the labour parties, India without Congress, would have developed differently. The crude determinist might argue that this is not so, or that these parties had to arise in the form which they took. But the important point about modern parties is that they are not simply reflections of their society. They have a life and dynamic of their own which is modified by the conditions in which they operate but not totally shaped by them.

The party remains the instrument sought by all social reformers, whether progressive or reactionary. It remains the main channel for political promotion in all but the least advanced nations. It provides the most important belief systems alternative to religion. It remains the most important single channel for mass pressure. It remains the most important single method of giving force to public opinion. It may be that the mass party of integration is passing away in modern society or even that the mass of the people is turning away from political participation altogether as individual rather than collective satisfaction becomes more important. The growth of bureaucracies impervious to partisan pressures makes the parties less important as centres of policy making. The spread of professionally managed mass media makes the primitive nineteenth-century methods of canvassing, holding meetings and distributing leaflets no longer necessary in advanced countries. Party workers, other than the technically accomplished, may become superfluous, especially where fund raising is not dependent on mass effort. At the other extreme of social complexity, in a number of underdeveloped countries the creation of parties was premature and they have been replaced by military or bureau-cratic élites. In the Communist states the mass movement has needed revitalisation and may even, in some countries, be facing the decline in cohesion and enthusiasm which has affected mass parties in affluent, competitive systems. The importance of party remains. It is a form of organisa-tion capable of infinite variation and adaptation. The parties are established institutions which will necessarily perpetuate themselves as long as they have any functions to fulfil. These functions may change and the manner of fulfilling them will also change. Party, the collective action of men to achieve political ends, must remain until either no one or everyone is prepared to take part in the political process.

Appendix: party systems

Party systems arranged in order of population and distinguished between effective and ineffective systems. Ineffective systems are normally suspended while military rule is imposed, but with a promise of a return to party rule. Ineffective systems are shown in brackets.

These categories are tentative and only tenable at the time of writing. Some are changing or have recently changed. It must not be implied that party systems placed in a category are similar in anything other than broad outlines and characteristics as explained in Chapter One.

COMPETITIVE SYSTEMS

Indistinct bi-partisan systems (where party structure is loosely associational or 'notable-led' and where programmatic differences are vague and the social composition of party leaderships similar):

United States, Brazil, Turkey, Philippines, South Korea, Iran, Canada, South Africa, Colombia, Sudan, (Greece), (Rwanda), Eire, Uruguay, El Salvador, (Burundi), Lebanon, (Sierra Leone), Nicaragua, Costa Rica, Panama, Lesotho, Gambia, Barbados.

Distinct bi-partisan systems (where parties are hierarchically structured, with marked programmatic differences and differently based leadership, membership and voting support):

Japan, West Germany, Britain, Australia, Sweden, Austria, Denmark, Norway, New Zealand, Jamaica, Trinidad, Guyana, Fiji, Mauritius, Malta.

Multi-party systems (where no party commands a clear majority and governments are normally composed of coalitions):

(Indonesia), (Nigeria), Italy, France, Argentina, (Congo Kinshasa), (South Vietnam), Netherlands, Peru, Ceylon, Belgium, Chile, Venezuela, Switzerland, (Ecuador), Finland, Guatemala, (Bolivia), Israel, (Laos), (South Yemen), (Cyprus), Luxemburg, Iceland.

Dominant-party systems (where one party dominates through elections with other parties allowed to function):

India, (Pakistan), Mexico, Morocco, Malaysia, Uganda, Malagasy, Tunisia, Zambia, Rhodesia, Paraguay, Singapore, Botswana.

NON-COMPETITIVE SYSTEMS

Broad one-party systems (where only one party or bloc is legal but contested elections may take place and open factionalism is allowed in the party):

Spain, Poland, Yugoslavia, Tanzania, Kenya, Cambodia, Cameroun, (Upper Volta), Ivory Coast, Malawi, Senegal, Niger, Somalia, Togo, Honduras, Liberia, Gabon.

Narrow one-party systems (where the party does not allow contests or factionalism and has a coherently expressed ideology):

Egypt, Burma, Taiwan, (Algeria), Portugal, (Iraq), Syria, Mali, Chad, Guinea, Mauritania, Congo Brazzaville.

Totalitarian systems (where the party is rigidly hierarchical, with a detailed ideology and effective control over all agencies of force, government and mass mobilisation):

China, Soviet Union, Romania, East Germany, North Vietnam, Czechoslovakia, North Korea, Hungary, Bulgaria, Cuba, Albania, Mongolia.

Non-party systems (including systems where parties have been abolished):

Thailand, Ethiopia, Afghanistan, Nepal, Ghana, Saudi Arabia, Yemen, Haiti, Dominican Republic, Dahomey, Jordan, Libya, Central African Republic, Kuwait, Persian Gulf Sheikhdoms.

Select bibliography

ALFORD, R. R. (1964), *Party and Society*, London: Murray.

ALMOND, G. A. and COLEMAN, J. S. (eds.) (1960), *The Politics of the Developing Areas*, Princeton University Press.

ARENDT, H. (1961), *The Origins of Totalitarianism*, London: Allen and Unwin.

BELL, D. (1960), *The End of Ideology*, Glencoe, Ill.: Free Press.

COLEMAN, J. S. and ROSBERG, C. G. (1964), *Political Parties and National Integration in Tropical Africa*, Berkeley: University of California Press.

DUVERGER, M. (1954), *Political Parties*, London: Methuen.

EINAUDI, M. *et al* (1951), *Communism in Western Europe*, Ithaca: Cornell University Press.

EINAUDI, M. and GOGUEL, F. (1952), *Christian Democracy in Italy and France*, Notre Dame, Ind.: University of Notre Dame Press.

ELDERSVELD, S. (1964), *Political Parties: a Behavioral Analysis*, Chicago: Rand McNally.

EULAU, H. (ed.) (1956), *Political Behaviour*, Glencoe, Ill.: Free Press.

FRIEDRICH, C. J. and BRZEZINSKI, Z. K. (1956), *Totalitarian Dictatorship and Autocracy*, Cambridge, Mass.: Harvard University Press.

HARRISON, S. (1960), *India—the Most Dangerous Decade*, Princeton University Press.

HEBERLE, R. (1951), *Social Movements*, New York: Appleton-Century-Crofts.

HODGKIN, T. L. (1961), *African Political Parties*, London: Penguin Books.

JENNINGS, W. I. (1960-62), *Party Politics*, London: Cambridge University Press.

JOHNSON, J. J. (1964), *Continuity and Change in Latin America*, Stanford University Press.

KAUTSKY, J. H. (1962), *Political Change in Underdeveloped Countries*, New York: Wiley.

KEY, V. O. (1954, 5th ed.), *Politics, Parties and Pressure Groups*, New York: Crowell.

KORNHAUSER, W. (1960), *The Politics of Mass Society*, London: Routledge & Kegan Paul.

LAIDLER, H. W. (1948), *Social and Economic Movements*, London: Routledge & Kegan Paul.

LANE, R. E. (1963), *Political Ideology*, New York: Free Press of Glencoe.

LA PALOMBARA, J. and WEINER, M. (1966), *Political Parties and Political Development*, Princeton University Press.

LASSWELL, H. D. and LERNER, D. (1965), *World Revolutionary Élites*, Cambridge, Mass.: M.I.T. Press.

LIPSET, S. M. (1960), *Political Man*, New York: Doubleday.

MACKENZIE, R. T. (1963), *British Political Parties*, London: Heinemann.

MAYO, C. G. and CROWE, B. L. (1966), *American Political Parties*, New York: Harper and Row.

MICHELS, R. (1958), *Political Parties*, Glencoe, Ill.: Free Press.

MILLEN, B. H. (1963), *The Political Role of Labour in Developing Countries*, Washington: Brookings Institute.

MONNEROT, J. (1953), *The Sociology of Communism*, London: Allen and Unwin.

NEUMANN, F. N. (1942), *Behemoth—the Structure and Practice of National Socialism*, London: Gollancz.

NEUMANN, S. (1956), *Modern Political Parties*, Chicago University Press.

OSTROGORSKI, N. I. (1902), *Democracy and the Organisation of Political Parties*, London: Macmillan.

SCHAPIRO, L. (1960), *The Communist Party of the Soviet Union*, London: Eyre and Spottiswoode.

SCHUMPETER, J. A. (1961, 3rd ed.), *Capitalism, Socialism and Democracy*, London: Allen and Unwin.

SELZNICK, P. (1952), *The Organisational Weapon*, New York: McGraw Hill.

SMELSER, N. J. (1962), *Theory of Collective Behaviour*, London: Routledge & Kegan Paul.

WARD, R. E. and RUSTOW, D. A. (1964), *Political Modernisation in Japan and Turkey*, Princeton University Press.

WEINER, M. (1957), *Party Politics in India*, Princeton University Press.